Principles of Fr[eedom]

Terence J. MacSwiney

Alpha Editions

This edition published in 2024

ISBN 9789362511331

Design and Setting By
Alpha Editions
www.alphaedis.com
Email - info@alphaedis.com

As per information held with us this book is in Public Domain.
This book is a reproduction of an important historical work.
Alpha Editions uses the best technology to reproduce historical work
in the same manner it was first published to preserve its original nature.
Any marks or number seen are left intentionally to preserve.

Contents

PREFACE - 1 -
CHAPTER I - 4 -
CHAPTER II - 8 -
CHAPTER III - 14 -
CHAPTER IV - 20 -
CHAPTER V - 27 -
CHAPTER VI - 34 -
CHAPTER VII - 43 -
CHAPTER VIII - 49 -
CHAPTER IX - 56 -
CHAPTER X - 61 -
CHAPTER XI - 65 -
CHAPTER XII - 69 -
CHAPTER XIII - 75 -
CHAPTER XIV - 80 -
CHAPTER XV - 84 -
CHAPTER XVI - 89 -
CHAPTER XVII - 92 -
CHAPTER XVIII - 97 -
CHAPTER XIX - 101 -

PREFACE

It was my intention to publish these articles in book form as soon as possible. I had them typed for the purpose. I had no time for revision save to insert in the typed copy words or lines omitted from the original printed matter. I also made an occasional verbal alteration in the original. One article, however, that on "Intellectual Freedom," though written in the series in the place in which it now stands, was not printed with them. It is now published for the first time.

RELIGION

I wish to make a note on the article under this heading to avoid a possible misconception amongst people outside Ireland. In Ireland there is no religious dissension, but there is religious insincerity. English politicians, to serve the end of dividing Ireland, have worked on the religious feelings of the North, suggesting the danger of Catholic ascendancy. There is not now, and there never was, any such danger, but our enemies, by raising the cry, sowed discord in the North, with the aim of destroying Irish unity. It should be borne in mind that when the Republican Standard was first raised in the field in Ireland, in the Rising of 1798, Catholics and Protestants in the North were united in the cause. Belfast was the first home of Republicanism in Ireland. This is the truth of the matter. The present-day cleavage is an unnatural thing created by Ireland's enemies to hold her in subjection and will disappear entirely with political Freedom.

It has had, however, in our day, one unhappy effect, only for a time fortunately, and this is disappearing. I refer to the rise of Hibernianism. The English ruling faction having, for their own political designs, corrupted the Orangemen with power and flattery, enabled them to establish an ascendancy not only over Ulster, but indirectly by their vote over the South. This becoming intolerable, some sincere but misguided Catholics in the North joined the organisation known as THE ANCIENT ORDER OF HIBERNIANS. This was, in effect, a sort of Catholic Freemasonry to counter the Orange Freemasonry, but like Orangeism, it was a political and not a religious weapon.

Further, as a political weapon, it extended all through Ireland during the last years of the Irish Parliamentary Movement. In Cork, for example, it completely controlled the city life for some years, but the rapid rise of the Republican Movement brought about the equally rapid fall of Hibernianism. At the present moment it has as little influence in the public life of Cork as Sir Edward Carson himself. The great bulk of its one-time members have joined the Republican Movement. This demonstrates clearly that anything in the nature of a sectarian movement is essentially repugnant to the Irish people. As I have pointed out, the Hibernian Order, when created, became at once a political weapon, but Ireland has discarded that, and other such weapons, for those with which she is carving out the destinies of the Republic. For a time, however, Hibernianism created an unnatural atmosphere of sectarian rivalry in Ireland. That has now happily passed away. At the time, however, of the writing of the article on Religion it was at its height, and this fact coloured the writing of the article. On re-

reading it and considering the publication of the present work I was inclined to suppress it, but decided that it ought to be included because it bears directly on the evil of materialism in religious bodies, which is a matter of grave concern to every religious community in the world.

T. MacS.

CHAPTER I

THE BASIS OF FREEDOM

I

Why should we fight for freedom? Is it not strange, that it has become necessary to ask and answer this question? We have fought our fight for centuries, and contending parties still continue the struggle, but the real significance of the struggle and its true motive force are hardly at all understood, and there is a curious but logical result. Men technically on the same side are separated by differences wide and deep, both of ideal and plan of action; while, conversely, men technically opposed have perhaps more in common than we realise in a sense deeper than we understand.

II

This is the question I would discuss. I find in practice everywhere in Ireland—it is worse out of Ireland—the doctrine, "The end justifies the means."

One party will denounce another for the use of discreditable tactics, but it will have no hesitation in using such itself if it can thereby snatch a discreditable victory. So, clear speaking is needed: a fight that is not clean-handed will make victory more disgraceful than any defeat. I make the point here because we stand for separation from the British Empire, and because I have heard it argued that we ought, if we could, make a foreign alliance to crush English power here, even if our foreign allies were engaged in crushing freedom elsewhere. When such a question can be proposed it should be answered, though the time is not ripe to test it. If Ireland were to win freedom by helping directly or indirectly to crush another people she would earn the execration she has herself poured out on tyranny for ages. I have come to see it is possible for Ireland to win her independence by base methods. It is imperative, therefore, that we should declare ourselves and know where we stand. And I stand by this principle: no physical victory can compensate for spiritual surrender. Whatever side denies that is not my side.

What, then, is the true basis to our claim to freedom? There are two points of view. The first we have when fresh from school, still in our teens, ready to tilt against everyone and everything, delighting in saying smart things— and able sometimes to say them—talking much and boldly of freedom, but satisfied if the thing sounds bravely. There is the later point of view. We are no longer boys; we have come to review the situation, and take a definite stand in life. We have had years of experience, keen struggles, not a little bitterness, and we are steadied. We feel a heart-beat for deeper things. It is no longer sufficient that they sound bravely; they must ring true. The schoolboy's dream is more of a Roman triumph—tramping armies, shouting multitudes, waving banners—all good enough in their way. But the dream of men is for something beyond all this show. If it were not, it could hardly claim a sacrifice.

III

A spiritual necessity makes the true significance of our claim to freedom: the material aspect is only a secondary consideration. A man facing life is gifted with certain powers of soul and body. It is of vital importance to himself and the community that he be given a full opportunity to develop his powers, and to fill his place worthily. In a free state he is in the natural environment for full self-development. In an enslaved state it is the reverse. When one country holds another in subjection that other suffers materially and morally. It suffers materially, being a prey for plunder. It suffers morally because of the corrupt influences the bigger nation sets at work to maintain its ascendancy. Because of this moral corruption national subjection should be resisted, as a state fostering vice; and as in the case of vice, when we understand it we have no option but to fight. With it we can make no terms. It is the duty of the rightful power to develop the best in its subjects: it is the practice of the usurping power to develop the basest. Our history affords many examples. When our rulers visit Ireland they bestow favours and titles on the supporters of their regime—but it is always seen that the greatest favours and highest titles are not for the honest adherent of their power—but for him who has betrayed the national cause that he entered public life to support. Observe the men who might be respected are passed over for him who ought to be despised. In the corrupt politician there was surely a better nature. A free state would have encouraged and developed it. The usurping state titled him for the use of his baser instincts. Such allurement must mean demoralisation. We are none of us angels, and under the best of circumstances find it hard to do worthy things; when all the temptation is to do unworthy things we are demoralised. Most of us, happily, will not give ourselves over to the evil influence, but we lose faith in the ideal. We are apathetic. We have powers and let them lie fallow. Our minds should be restless for noble and beautiful things; they are hopeless in a land everywhere confined and wasted. In the destruction of spirit entailed lies the deeper significance of our claim to freedom.

IV

It is a spiritual appeal, then, that primarily moves us. We are urged to action by a beautiful ideal. The motive force must be likewise true and beautiful. It is love of country that inspires us; not hate of the enemy and desire for full satisfaction for the past. Pause awhile. We are all irritated now and then by some mawkish interpretation of our motive force that makes it seem a weakly thing, invoked to help us in evading difficulties instead of conquering them. Love in any genuine form is strong, vital and warm-blooded. Let it not be confused with any flabby substitute. Take a parallel case. Should we, because of the mawkishness of a "Princess Novelette," deride the beautiful dream that keeps ages wondering and joyous, that is occasionally caught up in the words of genius, as when Shelley sings: "I arise from dreams of thee"? When foolish people make a sacred thing seem silly, let us at least be sane. The man who cries out for the sacred thing but voices a universal need. To exist, the healthy mind must have beautiful things—the rapture of a song, the music of running water, the glory of the sunset and its dreams, and the deeper dreams of the dawn. It is nothing but love of country that rouses us to make our land full-blooded and beautiful where now she is pallid and wasted. This, too, has its deeper significance.

V

If we want full revenge for the past the best way to get it is to remain as we are. As we are, Ireland is a menace to England. We need not debate this—she herself admits it by her continued efforts to pacify us in her own stupid way. Would she not ignore us if it were quite safe so to do? On the other hand, if we succeed in our efforts to separate from her, the benefit to England will be second only to our own. This might strike us strangely, but 'tis true, not the less true because the English people could hardly understand or appreciate it now. The military defence of Ireland is almost farcical. A free Ireland could make it a reality—could make it strong against invasion. This would secure England from attack on our side. No one is, I take it, so foolish as to suppose, being free, we would enter quarrels not our own. We should remain neutral. Our common sense would so dictate, our sense of right would so demand. The freedom of a nation carries with it the responsibility that it be no menace to the freedom of another nation. The freedom of all makes for the security of all. If there are tyrannies on earth one nation cannot set things right, but it is still bound so to order its own affairs as to be consistent with universal freedom and friendship. And, again, strange as it may seem, separation from England will alone make for final friendship with England. For no one is so foolish as to wish to be for ever at war with England. It is unthinkable. Now the most beautiful motive for freedom is vindicated. Our liberty stands to benefit the enemy instead of injuring him. If we want to injure him, we should remain as we are—a menace to him. The opportunity will come, but it would hardly make us happy. This but makes clear a need of the human race. Freedom rightly considered is not a mere setting-up of a number of independent units. It makes for harmony among nations and good fellowship on earth.

VI

I have written carefully that no one may escape the conclusion. It is clear and exacting, but in the issue it is beautiful. We fight for freedom—not for the vanity of the world, not to have a fine conceit of ourselves, not to be as bad—or if we prefer to put it so, as big as our neighbours. The inspiration is drawn from a deeper element of our being. We stifle for self-development individually and as a nation. If we don't go forward we must go down. It is a matter of life and death; it is out soul's salvation. If the whole nation stand for it, we are happy; we shall be grandly victorious. If only a few are faithful found they must be the more steadfast for being but a few. They stand for an individual right that is inalienable. A majority has no right to annul it, and no power to destroy it. Tyrannies may persecute, slay, or banish those who defend it; the thing is indestructible. It does not need legions to protect it nor genius to proclaim it, though the poets have always glorified it, and the legions will ultimately acknowledge it. One man alone may vindicate it, and because that one man has never failed it has never died. Not, indeed, that Ireland has ever been reduced to a single loyal son. She never will be. We have not survived the centuries to be conquered now. But the profound significance of the struggle, of its deep spiritual appeal, of the imperative need for a motive force as lofty and beautiful, of the consciousness that worthy winning of freedom is a labour for human brotherhood; the significance of it all is seen in the obligation it imposes on everyone to be true, the majority notwithstanding. He is called to a grave charge who is called to resist the majority. But he will resist, knowing his victory will lead them to a dearer dream than they had ever known. He will fight for that ideal in obscurity, little heeded—in the open, misunderstood; in humble places, still undaunted; in high places, seizing every vantage point, never crushed, never silent, never despairing, cheering a few comrades with hope for the morrow. And should these few sink in the struggle the greatness of the ideal is proven in the last hour; as they fall their country awakens to their dream, and he who inspired and sustained them is justified; justified against the whole race, he who once stood alone against them. In the hour he falls he is the saviour of his race.

CHAPTER II

SEPARATION.

I

When we plead for separation from the British Empire as the only basis on which our country can have full development, and on which we can have final peace with England, we find in opponents a variety of attitudes, but one attitude invariably absent—a readiness to discuss the question fairly and refute it, if this can be done. One man will take it superficially and heatedly, assuming it to be, according to his party, a censure on Mr. Redmond or Mr. O'Brien. Another will take it superficially, but, as he thinks, philosophically, and will dismiss it with a smile. With the followers of Mr. Redmond or Mr. O'Brien we can hardly argue at present, but we should not lose heart on their account, for these men move *en masse*. One day the consciousness of the country will be electrified with a great deed or a great sacrifice and the multitude will break from lethargy or prejudice and march with a shout for freedom in a true, a brave, and a beautiful sense. We must work and prepare for that hour. Then there is our philosophical friend. I expect him to hear my arguments. When I am done, he may not agree with me on all points; he may not agree with me on any point; but if he come with me, I promise him one thing: this question can no longer be dismissed with a smile.

II

Our friend's attitude is explained in part by our never having attempted to show that a separatist policy is great and wise. We have held it as a right, have fought for it, have made sacrifices for it, and vowed to have it at any cost; but we have not found for it a definite place in a philosophy of life. Superficial though he be, our friend has indicated a need: we must take the question philosophically—but in the great and true sense. It is a truism of philosophy and science that the world is a harmonious whole, and that with the increase of knowledge, laws can be discovered to explain the order and the unity of the universe. Accordingly, if we are to justify our own position as separatists, we must show that it will harmonise, unify and develop our national life, that it will restore us to a place among the nations, enable us to fulfil a national destiny, a destiny which, through all our struggles, we ever believe is great, and waiting for us. That must be accepted if we are to get at the truth of the matter. A great doctrine that dominates our lives, that lays down a rigid course of action, that involves self-denial, hard struggles, endurance for years, and possibly death before the goal is reached—any such doctrine must be capable of having its truth demonstrated by the discovery of principles that govern and justify it. Otherwise we cannot yield it our allegiance. Let us to the examination, then; we shall find it soul-stirring and inspiring. We must be prepared, however, to abandon many deeply-rooted prejudices; if we are unwilling, we must abandon the truth. But we will find courage in moving forward, and will triumph in the end, by keeping in mind at all times that the end of freedom is to realise the salvation and happiness of all peoples, to make the world, and not any selfish corner of it, a more beautiful dwelling-place for men.

Treated in this light, the question becomes for all earnest men great and arresting. Our friend, who may have smiled, will discuss it readily now. Yet he may not be convinced; he may point his finger over the wasted land and contrast its weakness with its opponents' strength, and conclude: "Your philosophy is beautiful, but only a dream." He is at least impressed; that is a point gained; and we may induce him to come further and further till he adopts the great principle we defend.

III

His difficulty now is the common error that a man's work for his country should be based on the assumption that it should bear full effect in his own time. This is most certainly false; for a man's life is counted by years, a nation's by centuries, and as work for the nation should be directed to bringing her to full maturity in the coming time, a man must be prepared to labour for an end that may be realised only in another generation. Consider how he disposes his plans for his individual life. His boyhood and youth are directed that his manhood and prime may be the golden age of life, full-blooded and strong-minded, with clear vision and great purpose and high hope, all justified by some definite achievement. A man's prime is great as his earlier years have been well directed and concentrated. In the early years the ground is prepared and the seed sown for the splendid period of full development. So it is with the nation: we must prepare the ground and sow the seed for the rich ripeness of maturity; and bearing in mind that the maturity of the nation will come, not in one generation but after many generations, we must be prepared to work in the knowledge that we prepare for a future that only other generations will enjoy. It does not mean that we shall work in loneliness, cheered by no vision of the Promised Land; we may even reach the Promised Land in our time, though we cannot explore all its great wonders: that will be the delight of ages. But some will never survive to celebrate the great victory that will establish our independence; yet they shall not go without reward; for to them will come a vision of soul of the future triumph, an exaltation of soul in the consciousness of labouring for that future, an exultation of soul in the knowledge that once its purpose is grasped, no tyranny can destroy it, that the destiny of our country is assured, and her dominion will endure for ever. Let any argument be raised against one such pioneer—he knows this in his heart, and it makes him indomitable, and it is he who is proven to be wise in the end. He judges the past clearly, and through the crust of things he discerns the truth in his own time, and puts his work in true relation to the great experience of life, and he is justified; for ultimately his work opens out, matures, and bears fruit a hundredfold. It may not be in a day, but when his hand falls dead, his glory becomes quickly manifest. He has lived a beautiful life, and has left a beautiful field; he has sacrificed the hour to give service for all time; he has entered the company of the great, and with them he will be remembered for ever. He is the practical man in the true sense. But there is the other self-styled practical man, who thinks all this proceeding foolish, and cries out for the expedient of the hour. Has he ever realised the promise of his proposals? No, he is the most inefficient person who has ever walked the earth. But for a saving consideration let him go contemplate the wasted efforts of the opportunist in every generation, and the broken projects scattered through the desert-places of history.

IV

Still one will look out on the grim things of the hour, and hypnotised by the hour will cry: "See the strength of the British Empire, see our wasted state; your hope is vain." Let him consider this clear truth: peoples endure; empires perish. Where are now the empires of antiquity? And the empires of to-day have the seed of dissolution in them. But the peoples that saw the old empires rise and hold sway are represented now in their posterity; the tyrannies they knew are dead and done with. The peoples endured; the empires perished; and the nations of the earth of this day will survive in posterity when the empires that now contend for mastery are gathered into the dust, with all dead, bad things. We shall endure; and the measure of our faith will be the measure of our achievement and of the greatness of our future place.

V

Is it not the dream of earnest men of all parties to have an end to our long war, a peace final and honourable, wherein the soul of the country can rest, revive and express itself; wherein poetry, music and art will pour out in uninterrupted joy, the joy of deliverance, flashing in splendour and superabundant in volume, evidence of long suppression? This is the dream of us all. But who can hope for this final peace while any part of our independence is denied? For, while we are connected in any shape with the British Empire the connection implies some dependence; this cannot be gainsaid; and who is so foolish as to expect that there will be no collision with the British Parliament, while there is this connection implying dependence on the British Empire? If such a one exists he goes against all experience and all history. On either side of the connection will be two interests—the English interest and the Irish interest, and they will be always at variance. Consider how parties within a single state are at variance, Conservatives and Radicals, in any country in Europe. The proposals of one are always insidious, dangerous or reactionary, as the case may be, in the eyes of the other; and in no case will the parties agree; they will at times even charge each other with treachery; there is never peace. It is the rule of party war. Who, then, can hope for peace where into the strife is imported a race difference, where the division is not of party but of people? That is in truth the vain hope. And be it borne in mind the race difference is not due to our predominating Gaelic stock, but to the separate countries and to distinct households in the human race. If we were all of English extraction the difference would still exist. There is the historic case of the American States; it is easy to understand. When a man's children come of age, they set up establishments for themselves, and live independently; they are always bound by affection to the parent-home; but if the father try to interfere in the house of a son, and govern it in any detail, there will be strife. It is hardly necessary to labour the point. If all the people in this country were of English extraction and England were to claim on that account that there should be a connection with her, and that it should dominate the people here, there would be strife; and it could have but one end—separation. We would, of whatever extraction, have lived in natural neighbourliness with England, but she chose to trap and harass us, and it will take long generations of goodwill to wipe out some memories. Again, and yet again, let there be no confusion of thought as to this final peace; it will never come while there is any formal link of dependence. The spirit of our manhood will always flame up to resent and resist that link. Separation and equality may restore ties of friendship; nothing else can: for individual development and general goodwill is the lesson of human life. We can be good neighbours, but most dangerous enemies, and in the coming time our hereditary foe cannot afford to have us on her flank. The present is promising; the future is developing for us: we shall reach the goal. Let us see to it that we shall be found worthy.

VI

That we be found worthy; let this be borne in mind. For it is true that here only is our great danger. If with our freedom to win, our country to open up, our future to develop, we learn no lesson from the mistakes of nations and live no better life than the great Powers, we shall have missed a golden opportunity, and shall be one of the failures of history. So far, on superficial judgment, we have been accounted a failure; though the simple maintenance of our fight for centuries has been in itself a splendid triumph.

But then only would we have failed in the great sense, when we had got our field and wasted it, as the nations around us waste theirs to-day. We led Europe once; let us lead again with a beautiful realisation of freedom; and let us beware of the delusion that is abroad, that we seek nothing more than to be free of restraint, as England, France and Germany are to-day; let us beware of the delusion that if we can scramble through anyhow to freedom we can then begin to live worthily, but that in the interval we cannot be too particular. That is the grim shadow that darkens our path, that falls between us and a beautiful human life, and may drive us to that tiger-like existence that makes havoc through the world to-day. Let us beware. I do not say we must settle now all disputes, such as capital, labour, and others, but that everyone should realise a duty to be high-minded and honourable in action; to regard his fellow not as a man to be circumvented, but as a brother to be sympathised with and uplifted. Neither kingdom, republic, nor commune can regenerate us; it is in the beautiful mind and a great ideal we shall find the charter of our freedom; and this is the philosophy that it is most essential to preach. We must not ignore it now, for how we work to-day will decide how we shall live to-morrow; and if we are not scrupulous in our struggle, we shall not be pure in our future state, I know there are many who are not indifferent to high-minded action, but who live in dread of an exacting code of life, fearing it will harass our movements and make success impossible. Let us correct this mistake with the reflection that the time is shaping for us. The power of our country is strengthening; the grip of the enemy is slackening; every extension of local government is a step nearer to independent government; the people are not satisfied with an instalment; their capacity for further power is developed, and they are equipped with weapons to win it. Even in our time have we made great advance. Let one fact alone make this evident. Less than twenty years ago the Irish language was despised; to-day the movement to restore it is strong enough to have it made compulsory in the National University. Can anyone doubt from this sign of the times alone that the hour points to freedom, and we are on the road to victory? That we shall win our freedom I have no doubt; that we shall use it well I am not so certain, for see how sadly misused it is abroad through the world to-day. That should be our final consideration, and we should make this a resolution—our future history shall be more glorious than that of any contemporary state. We shall look for prosperity, no doubt, but let our enthusiasm be for beautiful living; we shall build up our strength, yet not for conquest, but as a pledge of brotherhood and a defence for the weaker ones of the earth; we shall take pride in our institutions, not only as guaranteeing the stability of the state, but as securing the happiness of the citizens, and we shall lead Europe again as we led it of old. We shall rouse the world from a wicked dream of material greed, of tyrannical power, of corrupt and callous politics to the wonder of a regenerated spirit, a new and beautiful dream; and we shall establish our state in a true freedom that will endure for ever.

CHAPTER III

MORAL FORCE

I

One of the great difficulties in discussing any question of importance in Ireland is that words have been twisted from their original and true significance, and if we are to have any effective discussion, we must first make clear the meaning of our terms. Love of country is quoted to tolerate every insidious error of weakness, but if it has any meaning it should make men strong-souled and resolute in every crisis. Men working for the extension of Local Government toast "Ireland a Nation," and extol Home Rule as independence; but while there is any restraint on us by a neighbouring Power, acknowledged superior, there is dependence to that extent. Straightway, those who fight for independence shift their ground and plead for absolute independence, but there is no such thing as qualified independence; and when we abandon the simple name to men of half-measures, we prejudice our cause and confuse the issue. Then there is the irreconcilable—how is he regarded in the common cry? Always an impossible, wild, foolish person, and we frequently resent the name and try to explain his reasonableness instead of exulting in his strength, for the true irreconcilable is the simple lover of the truth. Among men fighting for freedom some start up in their plea for liberty, pointing to the prosperity of England, France, and Germany, and when we debate the means by which they won their power, we find our friends draw no distinction between true freedom and licentious living; but it would be better to be crushed under the wheels of great Powers than to prosper by their example. And so, through every discussion we must make clear the meaning of our terms. There is one I would treat particularly now. Of all the terms glibly flung about in every debate not one has been so confused as Moral Force.

II

Since the time of O'Connell the cry Moral Force has been used persistently to cover up the weakness of every politician who was afraid or unwilling to fight for the whole rights of his country, and confusion has been the consequence. I am not going here to raise old debates over O'Connell's memory, who, when all is said, was a great man and a patriot. Let those of us who read with burning eyes of the shameless fiasco of Clontarf recall for full judgment the O'Connell of earlier years, when his unwearied heart was fighting the uphill fight of the pioneer. But a great need now is to challenge his later influence, which is overshadowing us to our undoing. For we find men of this time who lack moral courage fighting in the name of moral force, while those who are pre-eminent as men of moral fibre are dismissed with a smile—physical-force men. To make clear the confusion we need only to distinguish moral force from moral weakness. There is the distinction. Call it what we will, moral courage, moral strength, moral force; we all recognise that great virtue of mind and heart that keeps a man unconquerable above every power of brute strength. I call it moral force, which is a good name, and I make the definition: a man of moral force is he who, seeing a thing to be right and essential and claiming his allegiance, stands for it as for the truth, unheeding any consequence. It is not that he is a wild person, utterly reckless of all mad possibilities, filled with a madder hope, and indifferent to any havoc that may ensue. No, but it is a first principle of his, that a true thing is a good thing, and from a good thing rightly pursued can follow no bad consequence. And he faces every possible development with conscience at rest—it may be with trepidation for his own courage in some great ordeal, but for the nobility of the cause and the beauty of the result that must ensue, always with serene faith. And soon the trepidation for himself passes, for a great cause always makes great men, and many who set out in hesitation die heroes. This it is that explains the strange and wonderful buoyancy of men, standing for great ideals, so little understood of others of weaker mould. The soldier of freedom knows he is forward in the battle of Truth, he knows his victory will make for a world beautiful, that if he must inflict or endure pain, it is for the regeneration of those who suffer, the emancipation of those in chains, the exaltation of those who die, and the security and happiness of generations yet unborn. For the strength that will support a man through every phase of this struggle a strong and courageous mind is the primary need—in a word, Moral Force. A man who will be brave only if tramping with a legion will fail in courage if called to stand in the breach alone. And it must be clear to all that till Ireland can again summon her banded armies there will be abundant need for men who will stand the single test. 'Tis the bravest test, the noblest test, and 'tis the test that offers the surest and greatest victory. For one armed man cannot resist a multitude, nor one army conquer countless legions; but not all the armies of all the Empires of earth can crush the spirit of one true man. And that one man will prevail.

III

But so much have we felt the need of resisting every slavish tendency that found refuge under the name of Moral Force, that those of us who would vindicate our manhood cried wildly out again for the physical test; and we cried it long and repeatedly the more we smarted under the meanness of retrograde times. But the time is again inspiring, and the air must now be cleared. We have set up for the final test of the man of unconquerable spirit that test which is the first and last argument of tyranny—recourse to brute strength. We have surrounded with fictitious glory the carnage of the battlefields; we have shouted of wading through our enemies' blood, as if bloody fields were beautiful; we have been contemptuous of peace, as if every war were exhilarating; but, "War is hell," said a famous general in the field. This, of course, is exaggeration, but there is a grim element of truth in the warning that must be kept in mind at all times. If one among us still would resent being asked to forego what he thinks a rightful need of vengeance, let him look into himself. Let him consider his feelings on the death of some notorious traitor or criminal; not satisfaction, but awe, is the uppermost feeling in his heart. Death sobers us all. But away from death this may be unconvincing; and one may still shout of the glory of floating the ship of freedom in the blood of the enemy. I give him pause. He may still correct his philosophy in view of the horror of a street accident or the brutality of a prize-fight.

IV

But war must be faced and blood must be shed, not gleefully, but as a terrible necessity, because there are moral horrors worse than any physical horror, because freedom is indispensable for a soul erect, and freedom must be had at any cost of suffering; the soul is greater than the body. This is the justification of war. If hesitating to undertake it means the overthrow of liberty possessed, or the lying passive in slavery already accomplished, then it is the duty of every man to fight if he is standing, or revolt if he is down. And he must make no peace till freedom is assured, for the moral plague that eats up a people whose independence is lost is more calamitous than any physical rending of limb from limb. The body is a passing phase; the spirit is immortal; and the degradation of that immortal part of man is the great tragedy of life. Consider all the mean things and debasing tendencies that wither up a people in a state of slavery. There are the bribes of those in power to maintain their ascendancy, the barter of every principle by time-servers; the corruption of public life and the apathy of private life; the hard struggle of those of high ideals, the conflict with all ignoble practices, the wearing down of patience, and in the end the quiet abandoning of the flag once bravely flourished; then the increased numbers of the apathetic and the general gloom, depression, and despair—everywhere a land decaying. Viciousness, meanness, cowardice, intolerance, every bad thing arises like a weed in the night and blights the land where freedom is dead; and the aspect of that land and the soul of that people become spectacles of disgust, revolting and terrible, terrible for the high things degraded and the great destinies imperilled. It would be less terrible if an earthquake split the land in two, and sank it into the ocean. To avert the moral plague of slavery men fly to arms, notwithstanding the physical consequence, and those who set more count by the physical consequences cannot by that avert them, for the moral disease is followed by physical wreck—if delayed still inevitable. So, physical force is justified, not *per se*, but as an expression of moral force; where it is unsupported by the higher principle it is evil incarnate. The true antithesis is not between moral force and physical force, but between moral force and moral weakness. That is the fundamental distinction being ignored on all sides. When the time demands and the occasion offers, it is imperative to have recourse to arms, but in that terrible crisis we must preserve our balance. If we leap forward for our enemies' blood, glorifying brute force, we set up the standard of the tyrant and heap up infamy for ourselves; on the other hand, if we hesitate to take the stern action demanded, we fail in strength of soul, and let slip the dogs of war to every extreme of weakness and wildness, to create depravity and horror that will ultimately destroy us. A true soldier of freedom will not hesitate to strike vigorously and strike home, knowing that on his resolution will depend the restoration and defence of liberty. But he will always remember that restraint is the great attribute that separates man from beast, that retaliation is the vicious resource of the tyrant and the slave; that magnanimity is the splendour of manhood; and he will remember that he strikes not at his enemy's life, but at his misdeed, that in destroying the misdeed, he makes not only for his own freedom, but even for his enemy's regeneration. This may be for most of us perhaps too great a dream. But for him who reads into the heart of the question and for the true shaping of his course it will stand; he will never forget, even in the thickest fight, that the enemy of to-day and yesterday may be the genuine comrade of to-morrow.

V

If it is imperative that we should fix unalterably our guiding principles before we are plunged unprepared into the fight, it is even more urgent we should clear the mind to the truth now, for we have fallen into the dangerous habit of deferring important questions on the plea that the time is not ripe. In a word, we lack moral strength; and so, that virtue that is to safeguard us in time of war is the great virtue that will redeem us in time of servility. It need not be further laboured that in a state enslaved every mean thing flourishes. The admission of it makes clear that in such a state it is more important that every evil be resisted. In a normal condition of liberty many temporary evils may arise; yet they are not dangerous—in the glow of a people's freedom they waste and die as disease dies in the sunlight. But where independence is suppressed and a people degenerate, a little evil is in an atmosphere to grow, and it grows and expands; and evils multiply and destroy. That is why men of high spirit working to regenerate a fallen people must be more insistent to watch every little defect and weak tendency that in a braver time would leave the soul unruffled. That is why every difficulty, once it becomes evident, is ripe for settlement. To evade the issue is to invite disaster. Resolution alone will save us in our many dangers. But a plea for policy will be raised to evade a particular and urgent question: "People won't unite on it"; that's one cry. "Ignorant people will be led astray"; that's another cry. There is always some excuse ready for evasion. The difficulty is, that every party likes some part of the truth; no party likes it all; but we must have it all, every line of it. We want no popular editions and no philosophic selections—the truth, the whole truth, and nothing but the truth. This must be the rule for everything concerning which a man has a public duty and ought to have a public opinion. There is a dangerous tendency gaining ground of slurring over vital things because the settlement of them involves great difficulty, and may involve great danger; but whatever the issue is we must face it. It is a step forward to bring men together on points of agreement, but men come thus together not without a certain amount of suspicion. In a fight for freedom that latent suspicion would become a mastering fear to seize and destroy us. We must allay it now. We must lead men to discuss points of difference with respect, forbearance, and courage, to find a consistent way of life for all that will inspire confidence in all. At present we inspire confidence in no one; it would be fatal to hide the fact. This is a necessary step to bringing matters to a head. We cannot hope to succeed all at once, but we must keep the great aim in view. There will be objections on all sides; from the *blasé* man of the world, concerned only for his comfort, the mean man of business concerned only for his profits, the man of policy always looking for a middle way, a certain type of religious pessimist who always spies danger in every proposal, and many others. We need not consider the comfort of the first nor the selfishness of the second; but the third and fourth require a word. The man of policy offers me his judgment instead of a clear consideration of the truth. 'Tis he who says: "You and I can discuss certain things privately. We are educated; we understand. Ignorant people can't understand, and you only make mischief in supposing it. It's not wise." To him I reply: "You are afraid to speak the whole truth; I am afraid to hide it. You are filled with the danger to ignorant people of having out everything; I am filled with the danger to *you* of suppressing anything. I do not propose to you that you can with the whole truth make ignorant people profound, but I say you must have the whole truth out for your own salvation." Here is the danger: we see life within certain limitations, and cannot see the possibly infinite significance of something we would put by. It is of grave importance that we see it rightly, and in the difficulties of the case our only safe course is to take the evidence life offers without prejudice and without fear, and write it down. When the matter is grave, let it be taken with all the mature deliberation and care its gravity demands, but once the evidence is clearly seen, let us for our salvation write it down. For any man to set his petty judgment above the need for setting down the truth is madness; and I refuse to do it. There is our religious pessimist to consider. To him I say I take religion more seriously. I take it not to evade the problems of life, but to solve them. When I tell him to have no fear, this is not my indifference to the issue, but a tribute to the faith that is in me. Let us be careful to do the right thing; then fear is inconsistent with faith. Nor can I understand the other attitude. Two thousand years after the preaching of the Sermon on the Mount we are to go about whispering to one another what is wise.

VI

To conclude: Now, and in every phase of the coming struggle, the strong mind is a greater need than the strong hand. We must be passionate, but the mind must guide and govern our passion. In the aberrations of the weak mind decrying resistance, let us not lose our balance and defy brute strength. At a later stage we must consider the ethics of resistance to the Civil Power; the significance of what is written now will be more apparent then. Let the cultivation of a brave, high spirit be our great task; it will make of each man's soul an unassailable fortress. Armies may fail, but it resists for ever. The body it informs may be crushed; the spirit in passing breathes on other souls, and other hearts are fired to action, and the fight goes on to victory. To the man whose mind is true and resolute ultimate victory is assured. No sophistry can sap his resistance; no weakness can tempt him to savage reprisals. He will neither abandon his heritage nor poison his nature. And in every crisis he is steadfast, in every issue justified. Rejoice, then good comrades; our souls are still our own. Through the coldness and depression of the time there has lightened a flash of the old fire; the old enthusiasm, warm and passionate, is again stirring us; we are forward to uphold our country's right, to fight for her liberty, and to justify our own generation. We shall conquer. Let the enemy count his dreadnoughts and number off his legions—where are now the legions of Rome and Carthage? And the Spirit of Freedom they challenged is alive and animating the young nations to-day. Hold we our heads high, then, and we shall bear our flag bravely through every fight. Persistent, consistent, straightforward and fearless, so shall we discipline the soul to great deeds, and make it indomitable. In the indomitable soul lies the assurance of our ultimate victory.

CHAPTER IV

BROTHERS AND ENEMIES

I

Our enemies are brothers from whom we are estranged. Here is the fundamental truth that explains and justifies our hope of re-establishing a real patriotism among all parties in Ireland, and a final peace with our ancient enemy of England. It is the view of prejudice that makes of the various sections of our people hopelessly hostile divisions, and raises up a barrier of hate between Ireland and England that can never be surmounted. If Ireland is to be regenerated, we must have internal unity; if the world is to be regenerated, we must have world-wide unity—not of government, but of brotherhood. To this great end every individual, every nation has a duty; and that the end may not be missed we must continually turn for the correction of our philosophy to reflecting on the common origin of the human race, on the beauty of the world that is the heritage of all, our common hopes and fears, and in the greatest sense the mutual interests of the peoples of the earth. If, unheeding this, any people make their part of the earth ugly with acts of tyranny and baseness, they threaten the security of all; if unconscious of it, a people always high-spirited are plunged into war with a neighbour, now a foe, and yet fight, as their nature compels them, bravely and magnanimously, they but drive their enemy back to the field of a purer life, and, perhaps, to the realisation of a more beautiful existence, a dream to which his stagnant soul steeped in ugliness could never rise.

II

On the road to freedom every alliance will be sternly tried. Internal friendship will not be made in a day, nor external friendship for many a day, and there will be how many temptations to hold it all a delusion and scatter the few still standing loyally to the flag. We must understand, then, the bond that holds us together on the line of march, and in the teeth of every opposition. Nothing but a genuine bond of brotherhood can so unite men, but we hardly seem to realise its truth. When a deep and ardent patriotism requires men of different creeds to come together frankly and in a spirit of comradeship, and when the most earnest of all the creeds do so, others who are colder and less earnest regard this union as a somewhat suspicious alliance; and, if they join in, do so reluctantly. Others come not at all; these think our friends labour in a delusion, that it needs but an occasion to start an old fear and drive them apart, to attack one another with ancient bitterness fired with fresh venom. We must combat that idea. Let us consider the attitude to one another of three units of the band, who represent the best of the company and should be typical of the whole; one who is a Catholic, one who is a Protestant, and one who may happen to be neither. The complete philosophy of any one of the three may not be accepted by the other two; the horizon of his hopes may be more or less distant, but that complete philosophy stretches beyond the limit of the sphere, within which they are drawn together to mutual understanding and comradeship, moved by a common hope, a brave purpose and a beautiful dream. The significance of their work may be deeper for one than for another, the origin of the dream and its ultimate aim may be points not held in common; but the beautiful tangible thing that they all now fight for, the purer public and private life, the more honourable dealings between men, the higher ideals for the community and the nation, the grander forbearance, courage and freedom, in all these they are at one. The instinctive recognition of an attack on the ideal is alive and vigilant in all three. The sympathy that binds them is ardent, deep and enduring. Observe them come together. Note the warm hand grasp, the drawn face of one, a hard-worker; of another, the eye anxious for a brother hard pressed; of the third, the eye glistening for the ideal triumphant; of all the intimate confidence, the mutual encouragement and self-sacrifice, never a note of despair, but always the exultation of the Great Fight, and the promise of a great victory. This is a finer company than a mere casual alliance; yet it makes the uninspired pause, wondering and questioning. These men are earnest men of different creeds; still they are as intimately bound to one another as if they knelt at the one altar. In the narrow view the creeds should be at one another's throats; here they are marching shoulder to shoulder. How is this? And the one whose creed is the most exacting could, perhaps, give the best reply. He would reply that within the sphere in which they work together the true thing that unites them can be done only the one right way; that instinctively seizing this right way they come together; that this is the line of advance to wider and deeper things that are his inspiration and his life; that if a comrade is roused to action by the nearer task, and labours bravely and rightly for it, he is on the road to widening vistas in his dream that now he may not see. That is what he would say whose vision of life is the widest. All objectors he may not satisfy. That what is life to him may leave his comrade cold is a difficulty; but against the difficulty stand the depth and reality of their comradeship, proven by mutual sacrifice, endurance, and faith, and he never doubts that their bond union will sometime prove to have a wise and beautiful meaning in the Annals of God.

III

But the men of different creeds who stand firmly and loyally together are a minority. We are faced with the great difficulty of uniting as a whole North and South; and we are faced with the grim fact that many whom we desire to unite are angrily repudiating a like desire, that many are sarcastically noting this, that many are coldly refusing to believe; while through it all the most bitter are emphasising enmity and glorifying it. All these unbelievers keep insisting North and South are natural enemies and must so remain. The situation is further embittered by acts of enmity being practised by both sides to the extreme provocation of the faithful few. Their forbearance will be sorely tried, and this is the final test of men. By those who cling to prejudice and abandon self-restraint, extol enmity, and always proceed to the further step—the plea to wipe the enemy out: the counter plea for forbearance is always scorned as the enervating gospel of weakness and despair. Though we like to call ourselves Christian, we have no desire for—nay even make a jest of—that outstanding Christian virtue; yet men not held by Christian dogma have joyously surrendered to the sublimity of that divine idea. Hear Shelley speak: "What nation has the example of the desolation of Attica by Mardonius and Xerxes, or the extinction of the Persian Empire by Alexander of Macedon restrained from outrage? Was not the pretext for this latter system of spoliation derived immediately from the former? Had revenge in this instance any other effect than to increase, instead of diminishing, the mass of malice and evil already existing in the world? The emptiness and folly of retaliation are apparent from every example which can be brought forward." Shelley writes much further on retaliation, which he denounces as "futile superstition." Simple violence repels every high and generous thinker. Hear one other, Mazzini: "What we have to do is not to establish a new order of things by violence. An order of things so established is always tyrannical even when it is better than the old." Let us bear this in mind when there is an act of aggression on either side of the Boyne. There will not be wanting on the other side a cry for retaliation and "a lesson." We shall receive every provocation to give up and acknowledge ancient bitterness, but then is the time to stand firm, then we shall need to practise the divine forbearance that is the secret of strength.

IV

But with only a minority standing to the flag we cry out for some hope of final success. Men will not fight without result for ever; they ask for some sign of progress, some gleam of the light of victory. Happily, searching the skies, our eyes can have their reward. We shall, no doubt, see, outstanding, dark evidence of old animosity; we shall hear fierce war-cries and see raging crowds, but the crowds are less numerous, and the wrath has lost its sting. Men who raged twenty years ago rage now, but their fury is less real; and young men growing up around them, quite indifferent to the ideal, are also indifferent to the counter cries: they are passive, unimpressed by either side. Rightly approached, they may understand and feel the glow of a fine enthusiasm; they are numbered by prejudice, they will become warm, active and daring under an inspiring appeal. Remember, and have done with despair. Think how you and I found our path step by step of the way: political life was full of conventions that suited our fathers' time, but have faded in the light of our day. We found these conventions unreal and put them by. This was no reflection on our fathers; what they fought for truly is our heritage, and we pay them a tribute in offering it in turn our loyalty inspired by their devotion. But their errors we must rectify; what they left undone we must take up and fulfil. That is the task of every generation, to take up the uncompleted work of the former one, and hand on to their successors an achievement and a heritage. Youth recognises this instinctively, and every generation will take a step in advance of its predecessor, putting by its prejudices and developing its truth. Every individual may know this from his own experience, and from it he knows that those who are now voicing old bitter cries are ageing, and will soon pass and leave no successors. Not that prejudice will die for ever. Each new day will have its own, but that which is now dividing and hampering us will pass. Let the memory of its bitterness be an incentive to checking new animosities and keeping the future safe; but in the present let us grasp and keep in our mind that the barrier that sundered our nation must crumble, if only we have faith and persist, undeterred by old bitter cries, for they are dying cries, undepressed by millions apathetic, for it is the great recurring sign of the ideal, that one hour its light will flash through quivering multitudes, and millions will have vision and rouse to regenerate the land.

V

Happily, it is nothing new to plead for brotherhood among Irishmen now; unhappily, it is not so generally admitted, nor even recognised, that the same reason that exists for restoring friendly relations among Irishmen, exists for the re-establishing of friendship with any outsider—England or another—with whom now or in the future we may be at war. Friendliness between neighbours is one of the natural things of life. In the case of individuals how beautifully it shows between two dwellers in the same street or townland. They rejoice together in prosperity; give mutual aid in adversity; in the ordinary daily round work together in a spirit of comradeship; at all times they find a bond of unity in their mutual interests. Consider, then, the sundering of their friendship by some act of evil on either side. The old friendship is turned to hate. Now the proximity that gave intimate pleasure to their comradeship gives as keen an edge to their enmity; they meet one another, cross one another, harass one another at every point. The bitterness that is such a poison to life must be revolting to their best instincts; deep in their hearts must be a yearning for the casting out of hate and the return of old comradeship. Still the estranged brothers are at daggers drawn. Sometimes the evil done is so great and the bitterness so keen that the old spirit can apparently never be restored; but while there is any hope whatever the true heart will keep it alive deep down, for it must be cherished and kept in mind if the whole beauty of life is to be renewed and preserved for ever. It is so with nations as with individuals. Once this is recognised we must be on guard against a new error, which is an old error in new form, the taking of means for end. The end of general peace is to give all nations freedom in essentials, to realise the deeper purpose, possibilities, fulness and beauty of life; it is not to have a peace at any price, peace with a certain surrender, the meaner peace that is akin to slavery. No, its message is to guard one nation from excess that has plunged another into evil, to leave the way open to a final peace, not base but honourable; it is to preserve the divine balance of the soul. It may be further urged that we are engaged in a great fight; that to try to rouse in men the more generous instincts will but weaken their hands by removing a certain driving bitterness that gives strength to their fight. Whatever it removes it will not be their strength. In a war admittedly between brothers, a civil war, where different conceptions of duty force men asunder, father is up against son, and brother against brother; yet they are not weakened in their contest by ties of blood and the deeper-lying harmony of things that in happier times prevail to the exclusion of bitterness and hate. When, therefore, you teach a man his enemy is in a deep sense his brother, you do not draw him from the fight, but you give him a new conception of the goal to win and with a great dream inspire him to persevere and reach the goal.

VI

If, then, beyond individual and national freedom there is this great dream still to be striven for, let us not decry it as something too sublime for earth. It must be our guiding star to lead us rightly as far as we may go. We can travel rightly that part of the road we now tread on only by shaping it true to the great end that ought to inspire us all. We shall have many temptations to swerve aside, but the power of mind that keeps our position clear and firm will react against every destroying influence. In the first stage of the fight for internal unity, when blind bigotry is furiously insisting that we but plan an insidious scheme for the oppression of a minority, our firmness will save us till our conception of the end grow on that minority and convince all of our earnestness. Then the dream will inspire them, the flag will claim them, and the first stage in the fight will be won. When internal unity is accomplished, we are within reach of freedom. Yes, but cries an objector, "Why plead for friendship with England, who will have peace only on condition of her supremacy?" And an answer is needed. If it takes two to make a fight, it also most certainly takes two to make a peace, unless one accepts the position of serf and surrenders. But this we do not fear; we can compel our freedom and we are confident of victory. There is still the step to friendship. Many will be baffled by the difficulty, that while we must keep alive our generous instincts, we must be stern and resolute in the fight; while we desire peace we must prosecute war; while we long for comradeship we must be breaking up dangerous alliances: literary, political, trades and social unions formed with England while she is asserting her supremacy must be broken up till they can be reformed on a basis of independence, equality and universal freedom. While we are prosecuting these vigorous measures it may not seem the way to final friendship; but we must persist; independence is first indispensable. Here again, however, while insisting among our own ranks on our conception of the end, it will grow on the mind of the enemy. They may put it by at first as a delusion or a snare, but one intimate moment will come when it will light up for them, and a new era is begun. In such a moment is evil abandoned, hate buried and friendship reborn. There is one honest fear that our independence would threaten their security: it will yet be replaced by the conviction that there is a surer safeguard in our freedom than in our suppression; the light will break through the clouds of suspicion and a star of stars will glorify the earth. For this end our enemy must have an ideal as high as our own; if thus an objector, he is right. But if in the gross materialism and greed of empire that is now the ruling passion with the enemy there is apparently little hope of a transformation that will make them spiritual, high-minded and generous, we must not abandon our ideal: while the meanness and tyranny of contemporary England stand forward against our argument and leave our reasoning cold, we can find a more subtle appeal in spirit, such an appeal as comes to us in a play of Shakespeare's, a song of Shelley's, or a picture of Turner's. From the heart of the enemy Genius cries, bearing witness to our common humanity, and the yearning for such high comradeship is alive, and the dream survives to light us on the forward path. We must travel that path rightly. We can so travel whatever the enemy's mind. More difficult it will be, but it can be done. That is the great significance and justification of Nationalism: it is the unanswerable argument to cosmopolitanism. If the greatness and beauty of life that ought to be the dream of all nations is denied by all but one, that one may keep alive the dream within her own frontier till its fascination will arrest and inspire the world. If this ultimate dream is still floating far off, in its pursuit there is for us achievement on achievement, and each brave thing done is in itself a beauty and a joy for ever. For the good fighter there is always fine recompense; a clear mind, warm blood, quick imagination, grasp of life and joy in action, and at the end of day always an eminence won. Yes, and from the height of that eminence will come ringing down to the last doubter a last word: we may reach the mountaintops in aspiring to the stars.

CHAPTER V

THE SECRET OF STRENGTH

I

To win our freedom we must be strong. But what is the secret of strength? It is fundamental to the whole question to understand this rightly, and, once grasped, make it the mainstay of individual existence, which is the foundation of national life. So much has the bodily power of over-riding minorities been made the criterion of absolute power, that to make clear the truth requires patience, insight, and a little mental study. But the end is a great end. It is to reconnoitre the most important battlefield, to discover the dispositions of the enemy, to measure our own resources and forge our strength link by link till we put on the armour of invincibility.

II

We have to grasp a distinction, knowledge of which is essential to discerning true strength. It can be clearly seen in the contrast between two certain fighting forces; first, a well-organised army, capably led, marching forward full of hope and buoyancy; second, a remnant of that army after disaster, a mere handful, not swept like their comrades in panic, but with souls set to fight a forlorn hope. Let us study the two: in the contrast we shall learn the secret. The courage of the well-organised army is not of so fine a quality as that nerving the few to fight to the last gasp. Consider first the army. What is its value as a force? Its discipline, its consolidation, the absolute obedience of its units to its officers, with the resulting unity of the whole; added to this is the sense of security in numbers, buoyancy of marching in a compact body, confidence in capable chiefs—all these factors go to the making of the courage and strength of the army. It is because their combination makes for the reliability of the force that discipline is so much valued and enforced, even to the point of death. Let us keep this in our mind, that their strength lies in their numbers, concentration, unity, reliance on one another and on their chiefs. A sudden disaster overtakes that army—the death of a great general, the miscarriage of some plan, a surprise attack, any of the chances of war, and the strength of the army is pierced, the discipline shaken, the sense of security gone. There is an instinctive movement to retreat; the habit of discipline keeps it orderly at first; the fear grows; all precaution and restraint are thrown aside—the retreat is a rout, the army a rabble, the end debacle. External discipline in giving them its strength left them without individual resource; internal discipline was ignored. When their combined strength was gone there was individual helplessness and panic. Consider, now, a remnant of that army, the members of which have the courage of the finer quality, individually resolute and set on resistance, clearly seeing at once all the possible consequences of their action, yet with that higher quality of soul accepting them without hesitation, pledging all human hopes for one last great hope of snatching victory from defeat, or, if not to save a lost battle, to check an advancing host, rally flying forces, and redeem a campaign. This is the heroic quality. In a crisis, the mind possessed of it does not wait for instructions or to reason a conclusion. It sees definite things, and swift as thought decides. There are flying legions, a flag down, a conquering army, and flight or death—to all eyes these are apparent; but to a brave company between that flight and death there is a gleam of hope, of victory, and for that forlorn hope flight is put by with the acceptance of death in the alternative if they fail. That is the quality to redeem us. Because it is witnessed so often in our history we are going to win; not for our prowess in more fortunate war on an even field or with the flowing tide, not for many victories in many lands, but for the sacred places in this our brave land that are memorable for fights that registered the land unconquerable. Why a last stand and a sacrifice are more inspiring than a great victory is one of the hidden things; but the truth stands: for thinking of them our spirits re-kindle, our courage re-awakens, and we stiffen our backs for another battle.

III

We have, then, to develop individual patience, courage, and resolution. Once this is borne in mind our work begins. In places there is a dangerous idea that sometime in the future we may be called on to strike a blow for freedom, but in the meantime there is little to do but watch and wait. This is a fatal error; we have to forge our strength in the interval. There is a further mistake that our national work is something apart, that social, business, religious and other concerns have no relation to it, and consequently we set apart a few hours of our leisure for national work, and go about our day as if no nation existed. But the middle of the day has a natural connection with the beginning of the day and the end of the day, and in whatever sphere a man finds himself, his acts must be in relation to and consistent with every other sphere. He will be the best patriot and the best soldier who is the best friend and the best citizen. One cannot be an honest man in one sphere and a rascal in another; and since a citizen to fulfil his duty to his country must be honourable and zealous, he must develop the underlying virtues in private life. He must strengthen the individual character, and to do this he must deal with many things seemingly remote and inconsequential from a national point of view. Everything that crosses a man's path in his day's round of little or great moment requires of him an attitude towards it, and the conscious or unconscious shaping of his attitude is determining how he will proceed in other spheres not now in view. Suppose the case of a man in business or social life. He has to work with others in a day's routine or fill up with them hours of leisure they enjoy together. Consider to what accompaniment the work is often done and with what manner of conversation the leisure is often filled. In a day's routine, where men work together, harmonious relations are necessary; yet what bickerings, contentions, animosities fill many a day over points never worth a thought. You will see two men squabble like cats for the veriest trifle, and then go through days like children, without a word. You will see something similar in social life among men and women equally—petty jealousies, personalities, slanderings, mean little stories of no great consequence in themselves, except in the converse sense of showing how small and contemptible everything and everyone concerned is. A keen eye notes with some depression the absence from both spheres of a fine manliness, a generous conception of things, a large outlook, that prevents a squabble with a smile, and because of a consciousness of the need for determination in a great fight for a principle, holds in true contempt the trivialities of an hour. For in all the mean little bickerings of life there is involved not a principle, but a petty pride. One has to note these things and decide a line of action. In the abstract the right course seems quite natural and easy, but in fact it is not so. A man finds another act towards him with unconscious impudence or arrogance, and at once flies into a rage; there is a fierce wrangle, and at the end he finds no purpose served, for nothing was at stake. He has lost his temper for nothing. In his heat he may tell you "he wouldn't let so-and-so do so-and-so," but on the same principle he should hold a street-argument with every fish-wife who might call him a name. He may tell you "he will make so-and-so respect him," but he offends his own self-respect if he cannot consider some things beneath him. One must have a sense of proportion and not elevate every little act of impudence into a challenge of life to be fought over as for life and death. It may be corrected with a little humour or a little disdain, but always with sympathy for the narrow mind whose view of life cannot reach beyond these petty things. Yet, to repeat, it is not easy. An irritable temper will be on fire before reason can check it; the process of correction will prove uncomfortable—the reasons will be there, but the feelings in revolt. Still, little by little, it is brought under, and in the end the nasty little irritability is killed just like a troublesome nerve; and, by and by, what once provoked a fierce rage becomes a subject for humorous reflection. Let no one fear we kill the nerve for the great Battle of Life; this we but strengthen and make constant. Every act of personal discipline is contributing to a subconscious reservoir whence our nobler energies are supplied for ever. And so, little things lead to great; and in an office wrangle or a social squabble there is need for developing those very qualities of judgment, courage, and patience which equip a man for the trials of the battlefield or the ruling of the state.

IV

We have considered the individual in business and social life. Let us now follow him into a political assembly. We find the same conditions prevail. Again, men fight bitterly but most frequently for nothing worth a fight; and again those rightly judging the situation must resolve not to be tempted into a wrangle even if their restraint be called by another name. What in a political assembly is often the first thing to note? We begin by the assumption, "this is a practical body of men," the words invariably used to cover the putting by of some great principle that we ought all endorse and uphold. But, first, by one of the many specious reasons now approved, we put the principle by, and before long we are at one another's throats about things involving no principle. It is not necessary to particularise. Note any meeting for the same general conditions: a chairman, indecisive, explaining rules of order which he lacks the grit to apply; members ignoring the chair and talking at one another; others calling to order or talking out of time or away from the point; one unconsciously showing the futility of the whole business by asking occasionally what is before the chair, or what the purpose of the meeting. This picture is familiar to us all, and curiously we seem to take it always as the particular freak of a particular time or locality; but it is nothing of the kind. It is the natural and logical result of putting by principle and trying to live away from it. Yet, that is what we are doing every day. It means we lack collectively the courage to pursue a thing to its logical conclusion and fight for the truth realised. If we are to be otherwise as a body, it will only be by personal discipline training for the wider and greater field. We must get a proper conception of the great cause we stand for, its magnitude and majesty, and that to be worthy of its service we must have a standard above reproach, have an end of petty proposals and underhand doings, be of brave front, resolute heart, and honourable intent. We must all understand this each in his own mind and shape his actions, each to be found faithful in the test. In fine, if in private life there is need for developing the great virtues requisite for public service, even more is it necessary in public life to develop the courage, patience and wisdom of the soldier and the statesman.

V

A concrete case will give a clearer grasp of the issue than any abstract reasoning. Our history, recent and remote, affords many examples of the abandoning by our public men of a principle, to defend which they entered public life; and our action on such an occasion is invariably the same—to regard the delinquent as simply a traitor, to load him with invective and scorn and brand him for ever. We never see it is not innate wickedness in the man, but a weakness against which he has been untrained and undisciplined, and which leaves him helpless in the first crisis. Ireland has recently been incensed by the action of some of her mayors and lord mayors in connection with the English Coronation festival; the feeling has been acute in the metropolis. Certain things are obvious, but how many see what is below the surface? Let me suggest a case and a series of circumstances; the more pointed the case, the more interesting. I will suppose a particular mayor is an old Fenian: let us see how for him a web is finely woven, and in the end how securely he is netted. First a mayor is a magistrate, and must take the judicial oath, but the old Fenian has taken an oath of allegiance to Ireland—clash number one. It is not simply a question of yes or no; there are attendant circumstances. Around a public man in place circulates a swarm of interested people, needy friends, meddling politicians, "supporters" generally. The chief magistrate will have influence on the bench which they all wish to invoke now and then, and they all wish to see him there. They don't approve of any principle that stands in the way. They group themselves together as his "supporters," and claiming to have put him into public life, they act as if they had acquired a lease of his soul. Not what he knows to be right, but what they believe to be useful, must be done; and before the first day is done the first fight must be made. However, the old Fenian has enough of the spirit of old times to come safe through the first round. But the second is close on his heels: Dublin Castle has been attentive. The mayor, as chief magistrate, has privileges on which the Castle now silently closes. There are private and veiled remonstrances by secret officials: "The mayor is acting illegally; he must not do so-and-so; such is the function of a magistrate; he has not taken the oath," etc. All this renewing the fight of the first day, for the Castle, too, wants the mayor on the bench to brand him as its own and alienate him from the old flag. It puts on the pressure by suppressing his privileges, weakening his influence, and disappointing his "supporters." All this is silently done. Still, the mayor holds fast, but he has not counted on this, and is beginning to be baffled and worried. Meanwhile a sort of guerilla attack is being maintained: invitations arrive to garden parties at Windsor, lesser functions nearer home, free passages to all the gay festivals, free admissions everywhere, the route indicated, and a gracious request for the presence of the mayor and mayoress. Genuine business engagements now save the situation, and the invitations are put by, but our chief citizen is now bewildered. These social missiles are flying in all directions, always gracious and flattering, never challenging and rude—who can withstand them? Still he is bewildered, but not yet caught. A new assault is made: the great Health Crusade Battery is called up. Here we must all unite, God's English and the wild Irish, the

Fenian and the Castleman, the labourer and the lord. Surely, we are all against the microbes. There is a great demonstration, their Excellencies attend—and the mayor presides. Under the banner of the microbe he is caught. It is a great occasion, which their Excellencies grace and improve. His Excellency is affable with the mayor; her Excellency is confidential and gracious with the mayoress—we might have been schoolchildren in the same townland we are so cordial. Everything proceeds amid plaudits, and winds up in acclamation. Their Excellencies depart. Great is the no-politics era—you can so quietly spike the guns of many an old politician—and keep him safe. The social amenities do this. Their Excellencies have gone, but they do not forget. There is a warm word of thanks for recent hospitality. Perhaps the mayor has a daughter about to be married, or a son has died; it is remembered, and the cordial congratulation or gracious sympathy comes duly under the great seal. What surly man would resent sympathy? And so, the strength of the old warrior is sapped; the web is woven finely; in its secret net the Castle has its man. You who have exercised yourselves in Dublin recently over mayoral doings, note all this—not to the making light of any man's surrender, but to the true judging of the event, its deeper significance and danger. Whoever fails must be called to account. When a man takes a position of trust, influence, and honour, and, whatever the difficulty, abandons a principle he should hold sacred, he must be held responsible. A battle is an ordeal, and we must be stern with friend and foe. But there is something more sinister than the weakness of the man: remember the net.

VI

The concrete case makes clear the principle in question. The man whom we have seen go down would have been safe if he had to fight no battle but one he could face with all his true friends, and in the open light of day. Having to fight a secret battle was never even considered: threats direct or vague or subtle, blandishments, cajolery, graciousness, patronage, flattery, plausible generalities, attacks indirect and insidious—all coming without pause, secret, silent, tireless. He who is to be proof against this, and above threat or flattery, must have been disciplined with the discipline of a life that trains him for every emergency. You cannot take up such a character like a garment to suit the occasion: it must be developed in private and public by all those daily acts that declare a man's attitude, register his convictions, and form his mind. It gives its own reward at once, even in the day where nothing is apparently at stake; where men scramble furiously over the petty things of life; for he who sees these things at their proper value is unruffled. His composure in all the fury has its own value. But the mind that held him so, by the very act of dismissing something petty, gets a clearer conception of the great things of life; by intuition is at once awake to a hovering and fatal menace to individual or national existence, unseen of the common eye; and in that hour proves, to the confusion of the enemy, clear, vigorous and swift. Let us, then, for this great end note what is the secret of strength. Not alone to be ready to stand in with a host and march bravely to battle—the discipline that provides for this is great and valuable and must be always observed and practised. This gives, however, only the common courage of the crowd, and can only be trusted on an even field where the chances of war are equal. But when there is a struggle to restore freedom, where from the nature of the case the chances are uneven and the soldiers of liberty are at every disadvantage, then must we seek to adjust the balance by a finer courage and a more enduring strength. The mustering of legions will not suffice. The general reviewing this fine array who would rightly estimate the power he may command, must silently examine the units, to judge of this brave host how large a company can be formed to fight a forlorn hope. If this spirit is in reserve, he is armed against every emergency. If the chances are equal, he will have a splendid victory; if by any of the turns of war his legions are shaken and disaster threatened, there is always a certain rallying-ground where the host can re-form and the field be re-won, and the flag that has seen so many vicissitudes be set at last high and proudly in the light of Freedom.

CHAPTER VI

PRINCIPLE IN ACTION

I

Our philosophy is valueless unless we bring it into life. With sufficient ingenuity we might frame theory after theory, and if they could not be put to the test of a work-a-day existence we but add another to the many dead theories that litter the History of Philosophy. Our principles are not to argue about, or write about, or hold meetings about, but primarily to give us a rule of life. To ignore this is to waste time and energy. To observe and follow it is to take from the clouds something that appeals to us, work it into life, by it interpret the problems to hand, make our choice between opposing standards, and maintain our fidelity to the true one against every opposition and through every fitful though terrible depression; so shall we startle people with its reality, and make for it a disciple or an opponent, but always at once convince the generation that there is a serious work in hand.

II

If our philosophy is to be worked into life the first thing naturally is to review the situation. If we are to judge rightly, we must understand the present, draw from the past its lesson, and shape our plans for the future true to the principles that govern and inform every generation. Let us survey the past, taking a sufficiently wide view between two points—say '98 and our own time—and we see certain definite conditions. Great luminous years—'98, '03, '48, '67, rise up, witness to a great principle, readiness for sacrifice, unshaken belief in truth, valour and freedom, and a flag that will ultimately prevail. In these years the people had vision, the blood quickened, a living flame swept the land, scorching up hypocrisy, deceit, meanness, and lighting all brave hearts to high hope and achievement—for, the whimperers notwithstanding, it was always achievement to challenge the enemy and stagger his power, though yet his expulsion is delayed. Between the glorious years of the living flame there intervened pallid times of depression, where every disease of soul and body crept into the open. True hearts lived, scattered here and there, believing still but disorganised and bewildered—the leaders were stricken down and in their place, obscuring the beauty of life, the grandeur of the past, and our future destiny, came time-servers, flatterers, hypocrites, open traffickers in honour and public decency, fastening their mean authority on the land. These are the two great resting-places in our historic survey: the generation of the living flame and the generation of despair; and it is for us to decide—for the decision rests with us—whether we shall in our time merely mark time or write another luminous chapter in the splendid history of our race.

III

Let us consider these two generations apart, to understand their distinctive features more clearly for our own guidance. Take first the years of vision and the general effort to replant the old flag on our walls. With the first enthusiasts breathing the living flame abroad, the kindling hope, the widening fires, the deepening dream, there grows a consciousness of the greatness of the goal, of the general duty, of the individual responsibility for higher character, steadier work, and purer motive; and gradually meanness, trickeries, and treacheries are weeded out of the individual and national consciousness: there is a realisation of a time come to restore the nation's independence, and with passion and enthusiasm are fused a fine resolve and nerve. All the excited doings of the feverish or pallid years are put by as unworthy or futile. The great idea inspires a great fight; and that fight is made, and, notwithstanding any reverse, must be recorded great. Whatever concourse of circumstances mar the dream and delay the victory, those brave years are as a torch in witness to the ideal, in justification of its soldiers and in promise of final success.

IV

Let us examine now the deadening years that intervene between the great fights for freedom. We have known something of these times ourselves, have touched on them already, and need not further draw out the demoralising things that corrupt and dishearten us. But what we urgently require to study is the kind of effort—more often the absence of effort—made in such years by those who keep their belief in freedom and feel at times impelled in some way or other to action. They have followed a lost battle, and in the aftermath of defeat they are numbed into despair. They refuse to surrender to the forces of the hour, but they lack the fine faith and enthusiasm of the braver years that challenged these forces at every point and stood or fell by the issue. They lie apathetic till, moved by some particular meanness or treachery, they are roused to spasmodic anger, rush to act in some spasmodic way—generally futile, and then relapse into helplessness again. They lack the vision that inspires every moment, discerns a sure way, and heightens the spirit to battle without ceasing, which is characteristic of the great years. They tacitly accept that theirs is a useless generation, that the enemy is in the ascendant, that they cannot unseat him, and their action, where any is made, is but to show their attitude, never to convince opponents that the battle is again beginning, that this is a bid for freedom, that history will be called on to record their fight and pay tribute to their times. Their action has never this great significance. When stung to fitful madness by the boastful votaries of power, their occasional frantic efforts are more as relief to their feelings than destructive to the tyranny in being. Let us realise this to the full; and seeing the futility in other years of every pathetic makeshift to annoy or circumvent the enemy, put by futilities and do a great work to justify our time.

V

We have, then, to consider and decide our immediate attitude to life, where we stand. There are errors to remove. The first is the assumption that we are only required to acknowledge the flag in places, offer it allegiance at certain meetings at certain times that form but a small part of our existence; while we allow ourselves to be dispensed from fidelity to our principles when in other places, where other standards are either explicitly or tacitly recognised. That we must carry our flag everywhere; that there must be no dispensation: these are the cardinal points of our philosophy. Life is a great battlefield, and any hour in the day a man's flag may be challenged and he must stand and justify it. An idea you hold as true is not to be professed only where it is proclaimed; it will whisper and you must be its prophet in strange places; it is insistent of all things—you must glory in it or deny it; there is no escaping it, and there is no middle way; wherever your path lies it will cross you and you must choose.

Beware lest on any plea you put it by. You cannot elect to do nothing; the concourse of circumstances would take you to some side; to do nothing is still to take a side. Priest, poet, professor, public man, professional man, business man, tradesman—everyone will be called to answer; in every walk of life the true idea will find the false in conflict and the battle must be fought out there—the battle is lost when we satisfy ourselves with an academic debate in our spare moments. This is a debating club age, and a plea for an ideal is often wasted, taken as a mere point in an argument; but to walk among men fighting passionately for it as a thing believed in, is to make it real, to influence men never reached in other ways; it is to arrest attention, arouse interest and quicken the masses to advance. And wherever the appeal for the flag is calling us the snare of the enemy is in wait. Our history so bristles with instances that a particular concrete case need not be cited. We know that priests will get more patronage if they discourage the national idea; that professors will get more emoluments and honours if they can ban it; that public men will receive places and titles if they betray it; that the professional man will be promised more aggrandisement, the business man more commerce, and the tradesman more traffic of his kind—if only he put by the flag. Most treacherous and insidious the temptation will come to the man, young and able, everywhere. It will say, "You have ability; come into the light—only put that by; it keeps you obscure. And what purpose does it serve now? Be practical; come." And you may weaken and yield and enter the light for the general applause, but the old idea will rankle deep down till smothered out, and you will stand in the splendour—a failure, miserable, hopeless, not apparent, indeed, but for all that, final. You may stand your ground, refuse the bribe, uphold the flag, and be rated a fool and a failure, but they who rate you so will not understand that you have won a battle greater than all the triumphs of empires; you will keep alive in your soul true light and enduring beauty; you will hear the music eternally in the heart of the high enthusiast and have vision of ultimate victory that has sustained all the world over the efforts of centuries, that uplifts the individual, consolidates the nation, and leads a wandering race from the desert into the Promised Land.

VI

If we are to justify ourselves in our time we must have done with dispensations. Many honest men are astray on this point and think attitudes justifiable that are at the root of all our failures. What is the weakness? It is so simple to explain and so easy to understand that one must wonder how we have been ignoring it quietly and generally so long. A man, as we have seen, acknowledges his flag in certain places; in other places it is challenged and he pulls it down. He is dispensed. He believes in his heart, may even write an anonymous letter to the paper, will salute the flag again elsewhere, but he will not carry his flag through every fight and through every day. When a particular crisis arises, which involves our public boards, public men, and business men in action, that requires a decision for or against the nation, he will find it in his place in life not wise to be prominent on his own side, and he is silently absent from his meetings—he gives a subscription but excuses himself from attendance. He satisfies himself with private professions of faith and whispered encouragement to those who fill the gap—words that won't be heard at a distance—and, worst of all, he thinks, because some stake in life may be jeopardised by bolder action, he is justified. The answer is, simply he is not justified. Nor should anyone who is prepared to take the risk himself take it on himself to absolve others—nor, least of all, openly preach a milder doctrine to lead others who are timid to the farther goal, believed in at heart. Encourage them by all means to practise their principles as far as they go; never restrict yours, or you will find yourself saying things you can't altogether approve; and if you tell a man to do things you can't altogether approve, and keep on telling him, it wears into you, and a thing you once held in abhorrence you come to think of with indifference. You change insensibly. Old friends rage at you, and because of it you rage at them—not knowing how you have changed. You dare not let what you believe lie in abeyance or say things inconsistent with it, else to-morrow you'll be puzzled to say what you believe. You will hardly say two things to fit each other. Let us have no half policies. Our policy must be full, clear, consistent, to satisfy the restless, inquiring minds; when we win all such over, the merely passive people will follow. It should be clear that no man can dispense himself or his fellow from a grave duty; but for all that we have been liberal with our dispensations, and it has left us in confusion and failure. On the understanding that we will be heroes to-morrow, we evade being men to-day. We think of some hazy hour in the future when we may get a call to great things; we realise not that the call is now, that the fight is afoot, that we must take the flag from its hidden resting-place and carry it boldly into life. So near a struggle may touch us with dread; but to dread provoking a fight is to endure without resistance all the consequences of a lost battle—a battle that might have been won. And if we are to be fit for the heroic to-morrow we must arise and be men to-day.

VII

At times we find ourselves on neutral ground. The exigencies of the struggle involve this; and unfortunately we have in our midst sincere men who do not believe in restoring Ireland to her original independence. Perhaps, from a tendency to lose our balance at times, it is well to have near by these men whose obvious sincerity may serve as a correcting influence. We have to make them one with us; in the meantime we meet them on neutral ground for some common purpose. Yet, we must take our flag everywhere? Yes, that is fundamental. What then of the places where men of diverging views meet; do we abjure the flag? By no means. The understanding here is not to force our views on others, but we must keep our principles clear in mind that no hostile view be forced on us. We must see to it that neutrality be observed. One of the pitfalls to be aware of is, that something which on our principles we should not recognise, is assumed as recognised by others because to attack it would be to violate neutrality. But if it may not be resisted, it may not be recognised; this is neutrality; it is to stand on equal terms. And since grave matters divide us—not directly concerned in our national struggle for freedom—let the dangerous idea be banished, that in entering on common ground we decry all opposing beliefs. For men who hold beliefs as vital it would not be creditable to either side to put them easily by. No, we do not ask them to forget themselves, but to respect one another—an entirely greater and more honourable principle. On neutral ground a man is not called on to abjure his flag; rather he and his flag are in sanctuary.

VIII

When we find the national idea touches life at every point, we begin to realise how frequent the call is to defend it without warning. It is not that men directly raise the idea purposely to reject it, but that their habit of life, to which they expect all to conform, is unconsciously assuming that our ruling principle can have no place now or in the future. Their assumption that the *status quo* cannot be changed will be the cause of most collision at first; and we must be quietly ready with the counter-assumption, stand for the old idea and justify it. We must realise, too, that the number of people who have definite, strong, well-developed views against ours are comparatively small. This small number embraces the English Government that commands forces, obeying it without reason, and influencing the general mass of people whose general attitude is indecision—adrift with the ruling force. It is this general mass of men we must permeate with the true idea, and give them more decision, more courage, more pride of race, and bring them to prove worthy of the race. They will begin to have confidence in the Cause when they begin to see it vindicated amongst them day by day; and that vindication must be our duty. That duty will not be to seek; it will offer itself and we shall have our test. How? Consider when men come together for any purpose where different views prevail and general things of no great moment form the subject of debate—suddenly, unconsciously or tentatively, one will raise some idea that may divide the company—say, acknowledging the English Crown in Ireland, putting by the claim for freedom, in the foolish hope of some material gain. There is much nonsense talked and confusion abroad on this head, and it is quite possible a man, believing in Ireland's full claim, will find himself in a large company who ought to stand for Ireland, yet who have lost a clear conception of her rights. But he will find that they have no clear conception the other way, either; they are confused and generally pliable; and so, when the challenging idea is introduced, if he is quick and clear with the vital points, he can tear the surface off the many nostrums of the hour and prove them mean, worthless, and degrading; and, doing so, he will be forming the minds about him. He must be ready; that is the great need. Understand how a conversation is often turned by a chance word, and how governed by one man who has passionate, well-defined views, while others are cold and undecided. Be that one man. You do not know where the circumstances of life will take you; your flag may be directly challenged to your face, and you must reveal yourself. These are things to avoid. Be firm, rather than aggressive; but be always quietly prepared for the aggressive man; that is to inspire confidence in the timid. Avoid vituperation as a disease, but have your facts clear and ready for friend or foe. Whenever, and wherever least expected, a false idea comes wandering forth, put in at once a luminous word or two to clear the air, hearten friends and keep them steady. If you find yourself alone in the midst of opponents, who assume you are with them and expect your co-operation, you put them right with a word. This will arrest them; they will understand where you stand, and that you are ready; and they will generally yield you respect. But whether it involve a fight or not, thus do you declare your attitude. We may conveniently call it—putting up the flag.

IX

It is well to consider something of the opposition that confronts a man who tries to fill his life with a brave purpose. He will be told it is an illusion; he is a dreamer, a crank, or a fool. And it may serve a purpose to see if our critics are blinded by no illusion, to contrast our folly with their wisdom. Here is one pushing by who will not be a fool, as he thinks—he's for the emigrant-ship. Ask yourself if the people who go out from the remote places of Ireland, quiet-spoken and ruddy-faced, and return after a few years loud-voiced and pallid, have found things exactly as their hope. They protest, yes; but their voice and colour belie them. Take the other man who does not emigrate but who has his fling at home, who "knocks around" and tells you to do likewise and be no fool—mark him for your guidance. You will find his leisure is boisterous, but never gay. Catch him between whiles off his guard and you will find the deadening lassitude of his life. This votary of pleasure has a burden to carry in whatever walk of life, high or low. On the higher plane he may have a more fastidious club or two, a more epicurean sense of enjoyment, more leisure and more luxury; but the type wherever found is the same. Life is an utter burden to him; in his soul is no interest, no inspiration, no energy, and no hope. Let him be no object of envy. Here a friend pats you on the shoulder: "Quite right; be neither an emigrant nor a waster; but be practical; have no illusions; deal with possibilities—who can say what is in the future? We must face these facts." Our confident friend lacks a sense of humour. He would put your plan by for its bearing on the future, but he proposes one himself that the future must justify. He tells you circumstances will not be in your favour: he assumes them in his own. But we only claim that our principles will rule the future as they have ruled the past; for the circumstances no man can speak. He calls you a dreamer for your principles, but he can't show, now nor in history, that his exemplars were ever justified. We are all dreamers, then; but some have ugly dreams, while the dreams of others are beautiful worlds, star-lighted and full of music.

X

Let the newborn enthusiast, just come eagerly to the flag, be warned of hours of depression that seize even the most earnest, the boldest and the strongest. Our work is the work of men, subject to such vicissitudes as hover around all human enterprise; and every man enrolled must face hard struggles and dark hours. Then the depression rushes down like a horrible, cold, dark mist that obscures every beautiful thing and every ray of hope. It may come from many causes: perhaps, a body not too robust, worn down by a tireless mind; perhaps, the memory of long years of effort, seemingly swallowed in oblivion and futility; perhaps contact with men on your own side whose presence there is a puzzle, who have no character and no conception of the grandeur of the Cause, and whose mean, petty, underhand jealousies numb you—you who think anyone claiming so fine a flag as ours should be naturally brave, straightforward and generous; perhaps the seemingly overwhelming strength of the enemy, and the listlessness of thousands who would hail freedom with rapture, but who now stand aloof in despair—and along with all this and intensifying it, the voice of our self-complacent practical friend, who has but sarcasm for a high impulse, and for an immutable principle the latest expedient of the hour. Through such an experience must the soldier of freedom live. But as surely as such an hour comes, there comes also a star to break the darkened sky; let those who feel the battle-weariness at times remember. When in places there may be but one or two to fight, it may seem of no avail; still let them be true and their numbers will be multiplied: love of truth is infectious. When progress is arrested, don't brood on what is, but on what was once achieved, what has since survived, and what we may yet achieve. If some have grown lax and temporise a little, with more firmness on your part mingle a little sympathy for them. It is harder to live a consistent life than die a brave death. Most men of generous instincts would rouse all their courage to a supreme moment and die for the Cause; but to rise to that supreme moment frequently and without warning is the burden of life for the Cause; and it is because of its exhausting strain and exacting demands that so many men have failed. We must get men to realise that to live is as daring as to die. But confusion has been made in our time by the glib phrase: "You are not asked now to die for Ireland, but to live for her," without insisting that the life shall aim at the ideal, the brave and the true. To slip apologetically through existence is not life. If such a mean philosophy went abroad, we would soon find the land a place of shivering creatures, without the capacity to live or the courage to die—calamity, surely. All these circumstances make for the hour of depression; and it may well be in such an hour, amid apathy and treachery, cold friends and active enemies, with worn-down frame and baffled mind, you, pleading for the Old Cause, may feel your voice is indeed a voice crying in the wilderness; and it may serve till the blood warms again and the imagination recover its glow, to think how a Voice, that cried in the wilderness thousands of years ago, is potent and inspiring now, where the voice of the "practical" man sends no whisper across the waste of years.

XI

What, then, to conclude, must be our decision? To take our philosophy into life. When we do that generally, in a deep and significant sense our War of Independence will have begun. Let there be no deferring a duty to a more convenient future. It is as possible that an opening for freedom may be thrust on us, as that we shall be required to organise a formal war with the usual movements of armies; in our assumptions for the second, let us not be guilty of the fatal error of overlooking the first. As in other spheres, so in politics we have our conventions; and how little they may be proven has been lately seen, when England went through a war of debate,[Footnote: Debate over House of Lords.] largely unreal, over her constitution and her liberties, even while foreign wars and complications were still being debated; and in the middle of it all, suddenly, from a local labour dispute, putting by all thought of the constitution, feeling as comparatively insignificant the fear of invasion, all England stood shuddering on the verge of frantic civil war;[Footnote: The Railway strike.] and all Ireland, when the moment of possible freedom was given, when England might have been hardly able to save herself, much less to hold us—Ireland, thinking and working in old grooves, lay helpless. Let us draw the moral. We cannot tell what unsuspected development may spring on us from the future, but we can always be prepared by understanding that the vital hour is the hour at hand. Let the brave choice now be made, and let the life around be governed by it; let every man stand to his colours and strike his flag to none; then shall we recover ground in all directions, and our time shall be recorded, not with the deadening but with the luminous years. In all the vicissitudes of the fight, let us not be distracted by the meanness of the mere time-server nor the treachery of the enemy, but be collected and cool; and remembering the many who are not with us from honest motives or unsuspected fears, live to show our belief beautiful and true and, in the eternal sense, practical. Then shall those who are worth convincing be held, and our difference may reduce itself to what is possible; then will they come to realise that he who maintains a great faith unshaken will make more things possible than the opportunist of the hour; then will they understand how much more is possible than they had ever dared to dream: they will have a vision of the goal; and with that vision will be born a steady enthusiasm, a clear purpose, and a resolute soul. The regeneration of the land will be no longer a distant dream but a shaping reality; the living flame will sweep through all hearts again; and Ireland will enter her last battle for freedom to emerge and reassume her place among the nations of the earth.

CHAPTER VII

LOYALTY

I

To be loyal to his cause is the finest tribute that can be paid to any man. And since loyalty to the Irish cause has been the great virtue of Irishmen through all history, it is time to have some clear thinking as to who are the Irish rebels and who the true men. When a stupid Government, grasping our reverence for fidelity, tried to ban our heroes by calling them felons, it was natural we should rejoin by writing "The Felons of our Land" and heap ridicule on their purpose. But once this end was achieved we should have reverted to the normal attitude and written up as the true Irish Loyalists, Brian the Great, and Shane the Proud, the valiant Owen Roe and the peerless Tone, Mitchel and Davis—irreconcilables all. When men revolt against an established evil it is their loyalty to the outraged truth we honour. We do not extol a rebel who rebels for rebellion's sake. Let us be clear on this point, or when we shall have re-established our freedom after centuries of effort it shall be open to every knave and traitor to challenge our independence and plot to readmit the enemy. Loyalty is the fine attribute of the fine nature; the word has been misused and maligned in Ireland: let us restore it to its rightful honour by remembering it to be the virtue of our heroes of all time. In considering it from this view-point we shall find occasion to touch on delicate positions that have often baffled and worried us—the asserting of our rights while using the machinery of the Government that denies them, the burning question of consistency, our attitude towards the political adventurer on one hand, and towards the honest man of half-measures on the other. Loyalty involves all this. And it shows that the man who revolts to win freedom is the same as he who dies to defend it. He does not change his face and nature with the changing times. He is loyal always and most wonderfully lovable, because in the darkest times, when banned as wild, wicked and rebelly, he is loyal still as from the beginning, and will be to the end. Yes, Tone is the true Irish Loyalist, and every aider and abettor of the enemy a rebel to Ireland and the Irish race.

II

When you insist on examining the question in the light of first principles your opportunist opponent at once feels the weakness of his position and always turns the point on your consistency. It is well, then, in advance to understand the relative value and importance of argument as argument in the statement of any case. A body of principles is primarily of value, not as affording a case that can be argued with ingenuity, but as enshrining one great principle that shines through and informs the rest, that illumines the mind of the individual, that warms, clarifies and invigorates—that, so to speak, puts the mind in focus, gets the facts of existence into perspective, and gives the individual everything in its right place and true proportion. It brings a man to the point where he does not dispute but believes. He has been wandering about cold and irresolute, tasting all philosophies, or none, and drinking deep despair. He does not understand the want in his soul while he has been looking for some panacea for its cure till the great light streams on him, and instead of receiving something he finds himself. That is it. There is a power of vision latent in us, clouded by error; the true philosophy dissipates the cloud and leaves the vision clear, wonderful and inspiring. He who acquired that vision is impervious to argument—it is not that he despises argument; on the contrary, he always uses it to its full strength. But he has had awakened within him something which the mere logician can never deduce, and that mysterious something is the explanation of his transformed life. He was a doubter, a falterer, a failure; he has become a believer, a fighter, a conqueror. You miss his significance completely when you take him for a theorist. The theorist propounds a view to which he must convert the world; the philosopher has a rule of life to immediately put into practice. His spirit flashes with a swiftness that can be encircled by no theory. It is his glory to have over and above a new penetrating argument in the mind—a new and wonderful vitality in the blood. The unbeliever, near by, still muddled by his cold theories, will argue and debate till his intellect is in a tangle. He fails to see that a man of intellectual agility might frame a theory and argue it out ably, and then suddenly turn over and with equal dexterity argue the other side. Do we not have set debates with speakers appointed on each side? That is dialectic—a trick of the mind. But philosophy is the wine of the spirit. The capacity then to argue the point is not the justification of a philosophy. That justification must be found in the virtue of the philosophy that gives its believer vision and grasp of life as a whole, that warms and quickens his heart and makes him in spirit buoyant, beautiful, wise and daring.

III

Let us come now to that burning question of consistency. "Very well, you won't acknowledge the English Crown. Why then use English coins and stamps? You don't recognise the Parliament at Westminster. Why then recognise the County Councils created by Bill at Westminster? Why avail of all the Local Government machinery?"—and so forth. The argument is a familiar one, and the answer is simple. Though no guns are thundering now, Ireland is virtually in a state of war. We are fighting to recover independence. The enemy has had to relax somewhat in the exigencies of the struggle and to concede all these positions of local government and enterprise now in question. We take these posts as places conceded in the fight and avail of them to strengthen, develop and uplift the country and prepare her to carry the last post. Surely this is adequate. On a field of battle it is always to the credit of a general to capture an enemy's post and use it for the final victory. It is a sign of the battle's progress, and tells the distant watchers on the hills how the fight is faring and who is going to win. There would be consternation away from the field only if word should come that the soldiers had gone into the tents of the enemy, acknowledging him and accepting his flag. That is the point to question. There can be no defence for the occupying of any post conceded by the enemy. It may be held for or against Ireland; any man accepting it and surrendering his flag to hold it stands condemned thereby. That is clear. Yet it may be objected that such a clear choice is not put to most of those undertaking the local government of Ireland, that few are conscious of such an issue and few governed by it. It is true. But for all that the machinery of local government is clearly under popular control, and as clearly worked for an immediate good, preparing for a greater end. Men unaware of it are unconsciously working for the general development of the country and recovering her old power and influence. Those conscious of the deeper issue enter every position to further that development and make the end obvious when the alien Government—finding those powers conceded to sap further resistance are on the contrary used to conquer wider fields—endeavours to force the popular government back to the purposes of an old and failing tyranny. That is the nature of the struggle now. At periods the enemy tries to stem the movement, and then the fight becomes general and keen around a certain position. In our time there were the Land Leagues, the Land War, fights for Home Rule, Universities, Irish; and these fights ended in Land Acts, Local Government Acts, University Acts, and the conceding of pride of place to the native language in university life. Every position gained is a step forward; it is accepted as such, and so is justified. For anyone who grasps the serious purpose of recovering Ireland's independence all along the line, the suggestion that we should abandon all machinery of local government and enterprise—because they are "Government positions"—to men definitely attached to the alien garrison is so foolish as not to be even entertained. When our attitude is questioned let it be made clear. That is the final answer to the man who challenges our consistency: we are carrying the trenches of the enemy.

IV

Even while dismissing a false idea of consistency we have to make clear another view still remote from the general mind. If we are to have an effective army of freedom we must enrol only men who have a clear conception of the goal, a readiness to yield full allegiance, and a determination to fight always so as to reflect honour on the flag. The importance of this will be felt only when we come to deal with concrete cases. While human nature is what it is we will have always on the outskirts of every movement a certain type of political adventurer who is ready to transfer his allegiance from one party to another according as he thinks the time serves. He has no principle but to be always with the ascendant party, and to succeed in that aim he is ready to court and betray every party in turn. As a result, he is a character well known to all. The honest man who has been following the wrong path, and after earnest inquiry comes to the flag, we readily distinguish. But it is fatal to any enterprise where the adventurer is enlisted and where his influence is allowed to dominate. It may seem strange that such men are given entry to great movements: the explanation is found in the desire of pioneers to make converts at once and convince the unconverted by the confidence of growing numbers. We ignore the danger to our growing strength when the adventurer comes along, loud in protest of his support—he is always affable and plausible, and is received as a "man of experience"; and in our anxiety for further strength we are apt to admit him without reserve. But we must make sure of our man. We must keep in mind that an alliance with the adventurer is more dangerous than his opposition; and we must remember the general public, typified by the man in the street whom we wish to convince, is quietly studying us, attracted perhaps by our principles and coming nearer to examine. If he knows nothing else, he knows the unprincipled man, and when he sees such in our ranks and councils he will not wait to argue or ask questions; he will go away and remain away. The extent to which men are ruled by the old adage, "Show me your company and I'll tell you what you are," is more widespread than we think. Moreover, consistency in a fine sense is involved in our decision. We fight for freedom, not for the hope of material profit or comfort, but because every fine instinct of manhood demands that man be free, and life beautiful and brave, and surely in such a splendid battle to have as allies mean, crafty profit-seekers would be amazing. Let us be loyal in the deep sense, and let us not be afraid of being few at first. An earnest band is more effective than a discreditable multitude. That band will increase in numbers and strength till it becomes the nucleus of an army that will be invincible.

V

The fine sense of consistency that keeps us clear of the adventurer decides also our attitude to the well-meaning man of half-measures. He says separation from England is not possible now and suggests some alternative, if not Home Rule, Grattan's Parliament, or leaving it an open question. In the general view this seems sensible, and we are tempted to make an alliance based on such a ground; and the alliance is made. What ensues? Men come together who believe in complete freedom, others who believe in partial freedom that may lead to complete freedom, and others who are satisfied with partial freedom as an end. Before long the alliance ends in a deadlock. The man of the most far-reaching view knows that every immediate action taken must be consistent with the wider view and the farther goal, if that goal is to be attained; and he finds that his ultimate principle is frequently involved in some action proposed for the moment. When such a moment comes he must be loyal to his flag and to a principle that if not generally acknowledged is an abiding rule with him; but his allies refuse to be bound by a principle that is an unwritten law for him because the law is not written down for them. This is the root of the trouble. The friends, thinking to work together for some common purpose, find the unsettled issue intrudes, and a debate ensues that leads to angry words, recriminations, bad feeling and disruption. The alliance based on half measures has not fulfilled its own purpose, but it has sown suspicion between the honest men whom it brought together; that is no good result from the practical proposal. There is an inference: men who are conscious of a clear complete demand should form their own plans, equally full of care and resolution, and go ahead on their own account. But we hear a plaintive cry abroad: "Oh, another split; that's Irishmen all over—can never unite," etc. We will not turn aside for the plaintive people; but let it be understood there can be an independent co-operation, where of use, with those honest men who will not go the whole way. That independent co-operation can serve the full purpose of the binding alliance that has proved fatal. Above all, let there be no charge of bad faith against the earnest man who chooses other ways than ours; it is altogether indefensible because we disagree with him to call his motives in question. Often he is as earnest as we are; often has given longer and greater service, and only qualifies his own attitude in anxiety to meet others. To this we cannot assent, but to charge him with bad faith is flagrantly unjust and always calamitous. In getting rid of the deadlock we have too often fallen to furiously fighting with one another. Let us bear this in mind, and concern ourselves more with the common enemy; but let not the hands of the men in the vanguard be tied by alien King, Constitution, or Parliament. All the conditions grow more definite and seem, perhaps, too exacting; remember the greatness of the enterprise. Suppose in the building of a mighty edifice the architect at any point were careless or slurred over a difficulty, trusting to luck to bring it right, how the whole building would go awry, and what a mighty collapse would follow. Let us stick to our colours and have no fear. When all these principles have been combined into one consistent whole, a light will flash over the land and the old spirit will be reborn; the mean will be purged of their meanness, the timid heartened with a fine courage, and the fearless will be justified: the land will be awake, militant, and marching to victory.

VI

This is, surely, the fine view of loyalty. Let us write it on our banners and proclaim it to the world. It is consistent, *honourable*, fearless and immutable. What is said here to-day with enthusiasm, exactness and care, will stand without emendation or enlargement, if in a temporary reverse we are called to stand in the dock to-morrow; or if, finely purged in the battle of freedom, we come through our last fight with splendid triumph, our loyalty is there still, shining like a great sun, the same beautiful, unchanging thing that has lighted us through every struggle—perhaps now to guide us in framing a constitution and giving to a world, distracted by kings, presidents and theorists, a new polity for nations. A waverer, half-caught between the light, half fearful with an old fear, pleads: "This is too much—we are men, not angels." Precisely, we are not angels; and because of our human weakness, our erring minds, our sudden passions, the most confident of us may at any moment find himself in the mud. What, then, will uplift him if he has been a waverer in principle as well as in fact? He is helpless, disgraced and undone. Let him know in time we do not set up fine principles in a fine conceit that we can easily live up to them, but in the full consciousness that we cannot possibly live away from them. That is the bed-rock truth. When the man of finer faith by any slip comes to the earth, he has to uplift him a staff that never fails, and to guide him a principle that strengthens him for another fight, to go forth, in a sense Alexander never dreamed of, to conquer new worlds. 'Tis the faith that is in him, and the flag he serves, that make a man worthy; and the meanest may be with the highest if he be true and give good service. Let us put by then the broken reed and the craft of little minds, and give us for our saving hope the banner of the angels and the loyalty of gods and men.

CHAPTER VIII

WOMANHOOD

*"And another said: I have married a wife and therefore
I cannot come."*

Yes, and we have been satisfied always to blame the wife, without noticing the man who is fond of his comfort first of all, who slips quietly away to enjoy a quiet smoke and a quiet glass in some quiet nook—always securing his escape by the readiest excuse. We are coming now to consider the aspect of the question that touches our sincere manhood; but let no one think we overlook that mean type of man who evades every call to duty on the comfortable plea: "I have married a wife."

I

When the mere man approaches the woman to study her, we can imagine the fair ones getting together and nudging one another in keen amusement as to what this seer is going to say. It is often sufficiently amusing when the clumsy male approaches her with self-satisfied air, thinking he has the secret of her mysterious being. I have no intention here of entering a rival search for the secret. But we can, perhaps, startle the gay ones from merriment to gravity by stating the simple fact that every man stands in some relationship to woman, either as son, brother, or husband; and if it be admitted that there is to be a fight to-morrow, then there are some things to be settled to-day. How is the woman training for to-morrow? How, then, will the man stand by that very binding relationship? Will clinging arms hold him back or proud ones wave him on? Will he have, in place of a comrade in the fight, a burden; or will the battle that has too often separated them but give them closer bonds of union and more intimate knowledge of the wonderful thing that is Life?

II

I wish to concentrate on one heroic example of Irish Womanhood that should serve as a model to this generation; and I do not mean to dwell on much that would require detailed examination. But some points should be indicated. For example, the awakening consciousness of our womanhood is troubling itself rightly over the woman's place in the community, is concentrating on the type delineated in "The Doll's House," and is agitating for a more honourable and dignified place. We applaud the pioneers thus fighting for their honour and dignity: but let them not make the mistake of assuming the men are wholly responsible for "The Doll's House," and the women would come out if they could. We have noticed the man who prefers his ease to any troubling duty: he has his mate in the woman who prefers to be wooed with trinkets, chocolates, and the theatre to a more beautiful way of life, that would give her a nobler place but more strenuous conditions. Again, the man is not always the lord of the house. He is as often, if not more frequently, its slave. Then there are the conventions of life. In place of a fine sense of courtesy prevailing between man and woman, which would recognise with the woman's finer sensibility a fine self-reliance, and with the man's greater strength a fine gentleness, we have a false code of manners, by which the woman is to be taken about, petted and treated generally as the useless being she often is; while the man becomes an effeminate creature that but cumbers the earth. Fine courtesy and fine comradeship go together. But we have allowed a standard to gain recognition that is a danger alike to the dignity of our womanhood and the virility of our manhood. It is for us who are men to labour for a finer spirit in our manhood: we cannot throw the blame for any weakness over on external conditions. The woman is in the same position. She must understand that greater than the need of the suffrage is the more urgent need of making her fellow-woman spirited and self-reliant, ready rather to anticipate a danger than to evade it. When she is thus trained, not all the men of all the nations can deny her recognition and equality.

III

For the battle of to-morrow then there is a preliminary fight to-day. The woman must come to this point, too. In life there is frequently so much meanness, a man is often called to acknowledge some degrading standard or fight for the very recognition of manhood, and the woman must stand in with him or help to pull him down. Let her understand this and her duty is present and urgent. The man so often wavers on the verge of the right path, the woman often decides him. If she is nobler than he, as is frequently the case, she can lift him to her level; if she is meaner, as she often is, she as surely drags him down. When they are both equal in spirit and nobility of nature, how the world is filled with a glory that should assure us, if nothing else could, of the truth of the Almighty God and a beautiful Eternity to explain the origin and destiny of their wonderful existence. They are indispensable to each other: if they stand apart, neither can realise in its fulness the beauty and glory of life. Let the man and woman see this, and let them know in the day that is at hand, how the challenge may come from some petty authority of the time that rules not by its integrity but by its favourites. We are cursed with such authority, and many a one drives about in luxury because he is obsequious to it: he prefers to be a parasite and to live in splendour than be a man and live in straits. He has what Bernard Shaw so aptly calls "the soul of a servant." If we are to prepare for a braver future, let us fight this evil thing; if we are to put by national servitude, let us begin by driving out individual obsequiousness. This is our training ground for to-morrow. Let the woman realise this, and at least as many women as men will prefer privation with self-respect to comfort with contempt. Let us, then, in the name of our common nature, ask those who have her training in hand, to teach the woman to despise the man of menial soul and to loathe the luxury that is his price.

IV

I wish to come to the heroic type of Irish Womanhood. When we need to hearten ourselves or others for a great enterprise, we instinctively turn to the examples of heroes and heroines who, in similar difficulties to ours, have entered the fight bravely, and issued heroically, leaving us a splendid heritage of fidelity and achievement. It is little to our credit that our heroes are so little known. It is less to our credit that our heroines are hardly known at all; and when we praise or sing of one our selection is not always the happiest. How often in the concert-hall or drawing-room do we get emotional when someone sings in tremulous tones, "She is far from the Land." There is a feeling for poetry in our lives, a feeling that patriotism will not have it, a melting pity for the love that went to wreck, a sympathy for ourselves and everybody and everything—a relaxing of all the nerves in a wave of sentiment. This emotion is of the enervating order. There is no sweep of strong fire through the blood, no tightening grip on life, no set resolve to stand to the flag and see the battle through. It is well, then, a generation that has heard from a thousand platforms, in plaintive notes, of Sarah Curran and her love should turn to the braver and more beautiful model of her who was the wife of Tone.

V

When we think of the qualities that are distinctive of the woman, we have in mind a finer gentleness, sensibility, sympathy and tenderness; and when we have these qualities intensified in any woman, and with them combined the endurance, courage and daring that are taken as the manly virtues, we have a woman of the heroic type. Of such a type was the wife of Tone. We can speak her praise without fear, for she was put to the test in every way, and in every way found marvellously true. For her devotion to, and encouragement of, her great husband in his great work, she would have won our high praise, even if, when he was stricken down and she was bereft of his wonderful love and buoyant spirits, she had proved forgetful of his work and the glory of his name. But she was bereft, and she was then found most marvellously true. Her devotion to Tone, while he was living and fighting, might be explained by the woman's passionate attachment to the man she loved. It is the woman's tenderness that is most evident in these early years, but there is shining evidence of the fortitude that showed her true nobility in the darker after-years. It was no ordinary love that bound them, and reading the record of their lives this stands out clear and beautiful. Tone, whom we know as patient organiser, tenacious fighter, far-seeing thinker, indomitable spirit—a born leader of men—writes to his wife with the passionate simplicity of an enraptured child: "I doat upon you and the babes." And his letters end thus: "Kiss the babies for me ten thousand times. God Almighty for ever bless you, my dearest life and soul." (This from the "French Atheist." I hope his traducers are heartily ashamed of themselves.) Nor is it strange. When, in the beginning of his enterprise, he is in America, preparing to go to France on his great mission, he is troubled by the thought of his defenceless ones. In the crisis how does his wife act? Does she wind clinging arms around him, telling him with tears, of their children and his early vows, and beseeching him to think of his love and forget his country? No; let the diary speak: "My wife especially, whose courage and whose zeal for my honour and interests were not in the least abated by all her past sufferings, supplicated me to let no consideration of her or our children stand for a moment in the way of my engagements to our friends and my duty to my country, adding that she would answer for our family during my absence, and that the same Providence which had so often, as it were, miraculously preserved us, would, she was confident, not desert us now." It is the unmistakable accent of the woman. She is quivering as she sends him forth, but the spirit in her eyes would put a trembling man to shame—a spirit that her peerless husband matched but no man could surpass. Her fortitude was to be more terribly tried in the terrible after-time, when the Cause went down in disaster and Tone had to answer with his life. No tribute could be so eloquent as the letter he wrote to her when the last moment had come and his doom was pronounced: "Adieu, dearest love, I find it impossible to finish this letter. Give my love to Mary; and, above all, remember you are now the only parent of our dearest children, and that the best proof you can give of your affection for me will be to preserve yourself for their education. God Almighty bless you all." That letter is like Stephens' speech from the dock, eloquent for what is left unsaid. There is no wailing for her, least of all for himself, not that their devoted souls were not on the rack: "As no words can express what I feel for you and our children, I shall not attempt it; complaint of any kind would be beneath your courage and mine"—but their souls, that were destined to suffer, came sublimely through the ordeal. When Tone left his children as a trust to his wife, he knew from the intimacy of their union what we learn from the after-event, how that trust might be placed and how faithfully it would be fulfilled. What a tribute from man to wife! How that trust was fulfilled is in evidence in every step of the following years. Remembering Tone's son who survived to write the memoirs was a child at his father's death, his simple tribute written in manhood is eloquent in the extreme: "I was brought up by my surviving parent in all the principles and in all the feelings of my father"—of itself it would suffice. But we can follow the years between and find moving evidence of the fulfilment of the trust. We see her devotion to her children and her proud care to preserve their independence and her own. She puts by patronage, having a higher title as the widow of a General of France; and she wins the respect of the great ones of France under the Republic and the Empire. Lucien Buonaparte, a year after Tone's death, pleaded before the Council of Five Hundred, in warm and eloquent praise: "If the services of Tone were not sufficient of themselves to rouse your feelings, I might mention the independent spirit and firmness of that noble woman who, on the tomb of her husband and her brother, mingles with her sighs aspirations for the deliverance of Ireland. I would attempt to give you an expression of that Irish spirit which is blended in her countenance with the expression of her grief. Such were those women of Sparta, who, on the return of their countrymen from the battle, when with anxious looks they ran over the ranks and missed amongst them their sons, their husbands, and their brothers, exclaimed, 'He died for his country; he died for the Republic.'" When the Republic fell, and in the upheaval her rights were ignored, she went to the Emperor Napoleon in person and, recalling the services of Tone, sought naturalization for her son to secure his career in the army; and to the wonder of all near by, the Emperor heard her with marked respect and immediately granted her request. She sought only this for her surviving son. She had seen two children die—there was moving pathos in the daughter's death—and now she was standing by the last. Never was child guarded more faithfully or sent more proudly on his path in life. One should read the memoirs to understand, and pause frequently to consider: how she promised her husband bravely in the beginning that she would answer for their children, and how, in what she afterwards styled the hyperbole of grief, she was called to fulfil to the letter, and was found faithful, with an unexampled strength and devotion; how she saw two children struck down by a fatal disease, and how she drew the surviving son back to health by her watchful care to send him on his college and military career with loving pride; how, when a Minister of France, irritated at her putting by his patronage, roughly told her he could not "take the Emperor by the collar to place Mr. Tone"—she went to the Emperor in person, with dignity but without fear, and won his respect; how the suggestion of the mean-minded that her demand was a pecuniary one, drew from her the proud boast that in all her misfortunes she had never learned to hold out her hand; how through all her misfortunes we watch her with wonderful dignity, delicacy, courage, and devotion quick to see what her trust demanded and never failing to answer the call, till her task is done, and we see her on the morning when her son sets out on the path she had prepared, the same quivering woman, who had sent her husband with words of comfort to his duty, now, after all the years of trial, sending her son as proudly on his path. It is their first parting. Let her own words speak: "Hitherto I had not allowed myself even to feel that my William was my own and my only child; I considered only that Tone's son was confided to me; but in that moment Nature resumed her rights. I sat in a field: the road was long and white before me and no object on it but my child.... I could not think; but all I had ever suffered seemed before and around me at that moment, and I wished so intensely to close my eyes for ever, that I wondered it did not happen. The transitions of the mind are very extraordinary. As I sat in that state, unable to think of the necessity of returning home, a little lark rushed up from the grass beside me; it whirled over my head and hovered in the air singing such a beautiful, cheering, and, as it sounded to me, approving note, that it roused me. I felt in my heart as if Tone had sent it to me. I returned to my solitary home." It is a picture to move us, to think of the devoted woman there in the sunshine, bent down in the grass, utterly alone, till the lark, sweeping heavenward in song, seems to give a message of gentle comfort from her husband's watching spirit. Our emotion now is of no enervating order. We are proud of our land and her people; our nerves are firm and set; our hearts cry out for action; we are not weeping, but burning for the Cause. How little we know of this heroic woman. We are in some ways familiar with Tone, his high character, his genial open nature, his daring, his patience, his farsightedness, his judgment—in spirit tireless and indomitable: a man peerless among his fellows. But he had yet one compeer; there was one nature that matched his to depth and height of its greatness—that nature was a woman's, and the woman was Wolfe Tone's wife.

VI

It is well this heroic example of our womanhood should be before not only our womanhood but our manhood. It should show us all that patriotism does not destroy the finer feelings, but rather calls them forth and gives them wider play. We have been too used to thinking that the qualities of love and tenderness are no virtues for a soldier, that they will sap his resolution and destroy his work; but our movements fail always when they fail to be human. Until we mature and the poetry in life is wakening, we are ready to act by a theory; but when Nature asserts herself the hard theorist fails to hold us. Let us remember and be human. We have been saying in effect, if not in so many words: "For Ireland's sake, don't fall in love"—we might as well say: "For Ireland's sake, don't let your blood circulate." It is impossible—even if it were possible it would be hateful. The man and woman have a great and beautiful destiny to fulfil together: to substitute for it an unnatural way of life that can claim neither the seclusion of the cloister nor the dominion of the world is neither beautiful nor great. We have cause for gratitude in the example before us. The woman can learn from it how she may equal the bravest man; and the man should learn to let his wife and children suffer rather than make of them willing slaves and cowards. For there are some earnest men who are ready to suffer themselves but cannot endure the suffering of those they love, and a mistaken family tenderness binds and drags them down. No one, surely, can hold it better to carefully put away every duty that may entail hardship on wife and child, for then the wife is, instead of a comrade, a burden, and the child becomes a degenerate creature, creeping between heaven and earth, afraid to hold his head erect, and unable to fulfil his duty to God or man. Let no man be afraid that those he loves may be tried in the fire; but let him, to the best of his strength, show them how to stand the ordeal, and then trust to the greatness of the Truth and the virtue of a loyal nature to bring each one forth in triumph, and he and they may have in the issue undreamed of recompense. For the battle that tries them will discover finer chords not yet touched in their intercourse; finer sympathies, susceptibilities, gentleness and strength; a deeper insight into life and a wider outlook on the world, making in fine a wonderful blend of wisdom, tenderness and courage that gives them to realise that life, with all its faults, struggles, and pain is still and for ever great and beautiful.

CHAPTER IX

THE FRONTIER

I

Our frontier is twofold, the language and the sea. For the majesty of our encircling waters we have no need to raise a plea, but to give God thanks for setting so certain a seal on our individual existence and giving us in the spreading horizon of the ocean some symbol of our illimitable destiny. For the language there is something still to be said; there are some ideas gaining currency that should be challenged—the cold denial of some that the unqualified name Irish be given to the literature of Irishman that is passionate with Irish enthusiasm and loyalty to Ireland, yet from the exigencies of the time had to be written in English; the view not only assumed but asserted by some of the Gael that the Gall may be recognised only if he take second place; the aloofness of many of the Gall, not troubling to understand their rights and duties; the ignoring on both sides of the fine significance of the name Irishman, of a spirit of patriotism and a deep-lying basis of authority and justice that will give stability to the state and secure its future against any upheaval that from the unrest of the time would seem to threaten the world.

II

Consider first the literature of Irishmen in English. From the attitude commonly taken on the question of literary values, it is clear that the primary significance of expression in writing is often lost. What is said, and the purpose for which it is said, take precedence of the medium through which it is said. But from our national awakening to the significance of the medium so long ignored we have grown so excited that we frequently forget the greater significance of the thing. The utterance of the man is of first importance, and, where his utterance has weight, the vital need is to secure it through some medium, the medium becoming important when one more than another is found to have a wider and more intimate appeal; and then we do well to become insistent for a particular medium when it is in anxiety for full delivery of the writer's thought and a wide knowledge of its truth. But we are losing sight of this natural order of things. It is well, then, the unconvinced Gall should hear why he should accept the Irish language; not simply to defer to the Gael, but to quicken the mind and defend the territory of what is now the common country of the Gael and Gall. Davis caught up the great significance of the language when he said: "Tis a surer barrier, and more important frontier, than fortress or river."

The language is at once our frontier and our first fortress, and behind it all Irishmen should stand, not because a particular branch of our people evolved it, but because it is the common heritage of all. One who has a knowledge of Irish can easily get evidence of its quickening power on the Irish mind. Travel in an Irish-speaking district and hail one of its old people in English, and you get in response a dull "Good-day, Sir." Salute him in Irish and you touch a secret spring. The dull eyes light up, the face is all animation, the body alert, and for a dull "good-day," you get warm benedictions, lively sallies, and after you, as you pass on your road, a flood of rich and racy Irish comes pouring down the wind. That is the secret power of the language. It makes the old men proud of their youth and gives to the young quickened faculties, an awakened imagination and a world to conquer. This is no exaggeration. It is not always obvious, because we do not touch the secret spring nor wander near the magic. But the truth is there to find for him who cares to search. You discover behind the dullness of a provincial town a bright centre of interest, and when you study the circle you know that here is some wonderful thing: priests, doctors, lawyers, teachers, tradesmen, clerks—all drawn together, young and old, both sexes, all enthusiasts. Sometimes a priest is teaching a smith, sometimes the smith is teaching the priest: for a moment at least we have unconsciously levelled barriers and there is jubilation in the natural life re-born. Out of that quickened life and consciousness rises a vivid imagination with a rush of thought and a power of expression that gives the nation a new literature. That is the justification of the language. It awakens and draws to expression minds that would otherwise be blank. It is not that the revelation of Davis is of less value than we think, but that through the medium of Irish other revelations will be won that would otherwise be lost. Again, in subtle ways we cannot wholly understand, it gives the Irish mind a defence against every other mind, taking in comradeship whatever good the others have to offer, while retaining its own power and place. The Irish mind can do itself justice only in Irish. But still some ardent and faithful spirits broke through every difficulty of time and circumstance and found expression in English, and we have the treasures of Davis, Mitchel, and Mangan; yet, the majority remained cold, and now, to quicken the mass, we turn to the old language. But this is not to decry what was won in other fields. In the widening future that beckons to us, we shall, if anything, give greater praise to these good fighters and enthusiasts, who in darker years, even with the language of the enemy, resisted his march and held the gap for Ireland.

III

On this ground the Gael and Gall stand on footing of equality. That is the point many on both sides miss and we need to emphasise it. Some Irishmen not of Gaelic stock speak of Irish as foreign to them, and would maintain English in the principal place now and in the future. We do well then to make clear to such a one that he is asked to adopt the language for Ireland's sake as a nation and for his own sake as a citizen. If he wishes to serve her he must stand for the language; if he prefers English civilisation he should go back to England. There only can he develop on English lines. An Irishman in Ireland with an English mind is a queer contradiction, who can serve neither Ireland nor England in any good sense, and both Ireland and England disown him. So the Irishman of other than Gaelic ancestors should stand in with us, not accepting something disagreeable as inevitable, but claiming a right by birth and citizenship, joining the fine army of the nation for a brave adventurous future, full of fine possibility and guaranteed by a fine comradeship—owning a land not of flattery and favouritism, but of freedom and manhood. This saving ideal has been often obscured by our sundering class names. This is why we would substitute as common for all the fine name of Irishman.

IV

But in asking all parties to accept the common name of Irishman, we find a fear rather suggested than declared—that men may be asked in this name to put by something they hold as a great principle of Life; that Catholic, Protestant and Dissenter will all be asked to find agreement in a fourth alternative, in which they will not submit to one another but will all equally belie themselves. There is such a hidden fear, and we should have it out and dispose of it. The best men of all parties will have no truck with this and they are right. But on what ground, then, shall we find agreement, the recognition of which Irish Citizenship implies? On this, that the man of whatever sincere principles, religious or civic, counts among his great duties his duty as citizen; and he defends his creed because he believes it to be a safe guide to the fulfilling of all duties, this including. When, therefore, we ask him to stand in as Irish Citizen, it is not that he is to abandon in one iota his sincere principles, but that he is to give us proof of his sincerity. He tells us his creed requires him to be a good citizen: we give him a fine field in which he can be to us a fine example.

V

In further consideration of this we should put by the thought of finding a mere working agreement. There is a deep-lying basis of authority and justice to seek, which it should be our highest aim to discover. Modern governments concede justice to those who can compel justice—even the democracy requires that you be strong enough to formulate a claim and sustain it; but this is the way of tyranny. A perfect government should seek, while careful to develop its stronger forces and keep them in perfect balance, to consider also the claims of those less powerful but not less true.

A government that over-rides the weak because it is safe, is a tyranny, and tyranny is in seed in the democratic governments of our time. We must consider this well, for it is pressing and grave; and we must get men to come together as citizens to defend the rights as well of the unit which is unsupported as of the party that commands great power. So shall we give steadiness and fervour to our growing strength by balancing it with truth and justice: so shall we found a government that excesses cannot undermine nor tyranny destroy.

VI

We have to consider, in conclusion, the unrest in the world, the war of parties and classes, and the need of judging the tendencies of the time to set our steps aright. With the wars and rumours of wars that threaten the great nations from without and the wild upheavals that threaten them within, it would be foolish to hide from ourselves the drift of events. We must decide our attitude; and if it is too much to hope that we may keep clear of the upheavals, we should aim at strengthening ourselves against the coming crash. We cannot set the world right, but we can go a long way to setting things in our own land right, by making through a common patriotism a united people. What if we are held up occasionally by the cold cries shot at every high aim—"dreamer—Utopia"; cry this in return: no vision of the dreamer can be more wild than the frantic make-shifts of the Great Powers to vie in armaments with one another or repress internal revolts. Consider England in the late strike that paralysed her. It was only suspended by a step that merely deferred the struggle; the strife is again threatening. All the powers are so threatened and their efforts to defer the hour are equally feverish and fruitless; for the hour is pressing and may flash on the world when 'tis least prepared. Let who will deride us, but let us prepare. We may not guide our steps with the certainty of prophets, nor hope by our beautiful schemes to make a perfect state; but we can only come near to perfection in the light of a perfect ideal, and however far below it we may remain, we can at least, under its inspiration, reach an existence rational and human: our justification for a brave effort lies in that the governments of this time are neither one nor the other. He who thinks Ireland's struggle to express her own mind, to give utterance to her own tongue, to stand behind her own frontier, is but a sentiment will be surprised to find it leads him to this point. Herein is the justification and the strength of the movement. Men are deriding things around them, of the significance of which they have not the remotest idea. Ireland is calling her children to a common banner, to the defence of her frontier, to the building up of a national life, harmonious and beautiful—a conception of citizenship, from which a right is conceded, not because it can be compelled, but because it is just: to the foundation of a state that will by its defence of the least powerful prove all powerful, that will be strong because true, beautiful because free, full of the music of her olden speech and caught by the magic of her encircling sea.

CHAPTER X

LITERATURE AND FREEDOM—THE PROPAGANDIST PLAYWRIGHT

I

A nation's literature is an index to its mind. If the nation has its freedom to win, from its literature may we learn if it is passionately in earnest in the fight, or if it is half-hearted, or if it cares not at all. Whatever state prevails, passionate men can pour their passion through literature to the nation's soul and make it burn and move and fight. For this reason it is of transcendent importance to the Cause. Literature is the Shrine of Freedom, its fortress, its banner, its charter. In its great temple patriots worship; from it soldiers go forth, wave its challenge, and fight, and conquering, write the charter of their country. Its great power is contested by none; rather, all recognise it, and many and violent are the disputes as to its right use and purpose. I propose to consider two of the disputants—the propagandist playwright and the art-for-art's-sake artist, since they raise issues that are our concern. It is curious that two so violently opposed should be so nearly alike in error: they are both afraid of life. The propagandist is all for one side; the artist afraid of every side. The one lacks imagination; the other lacks heart; they are both wide of the truth. The service of the truth requires them to pursue one course; in their dispute they swerve from that course, one to right, one to left. Because they leave the path on opposite sides, they do not see how much alike is their error; but that they do both leave the path is my point, and it is well we should consider it. It would be difficult to deal with both sides at once; so I will consider the propagandist first. What I have to charge against him is that his work is insincere, that he is afraid to do justice to the other side, that he makes ridicule of our exemplars, that he helps to keep the *poseur* in being; and to conclude, that only by a saving sense of humour can we find our way back to the truth.

II

When we judge literature we do so by reference to the eternal truth, not by what the writer considers the present phase of truth; and if literature so tested is found guilty of suppression, evasion or misinterpretation, we call the work insincere, though the author may have written in perfect good faith. That is a necessary distinction to keep in mind. If you call a man's work insincere, the superficial critic will take it as calling the man himself insincere; but the two are distinct, and it needs to be emphasised, for sincere men are making these propagandist plays, of which the manifest and glaring untruth is working mischief to the national mind. A type of such a play is familiar enough in these days when we like to ridicule the West Briton. We are served up puppets representing the shoneen with a lisp set over against the patriot who says all the proper things suitable to the occasion. Now, such a play serves no good purpose, but it has a certain bad effect. It does not give a true interpretation of life; it enlightens no one; but it flatters the prejudices of people who profess things for which they have no zeal. That is the root of the mischief. Many of us will readily profess a principle for which we will not as readily suffer, but when the pinch comes and we are asked to do service for the flag, we cover our unwillingness by calling the man on the other side names. Where such a spirit prevails there can be no national awakening. If we put a play before the people, it must be with a hope of arresting attention, striking their imagination, giving them a grip of reality, and filling them with a joy in life. Now, the propagandist play does none of these things; it has neither joy nor reality; its characters are puppets and ridiculous; they are essentially caricatures. This is supposed to convert the unbeliever; but the intelligent unbeliever coming to it is either bored or irritated by its extravagant absurdity, and if he admits our sincerity, it is only at the expense of our intelligence.

III

A propagandist play for a political end is even more mischievous—at least lovers of freedom have more cause for protest. It makes our heroes ridiculous. No man of imagination can stand these impossible persons of the play who "walk on" eternally talking of Ireland. Our heroes were men; these are *poseurs*. Get to understand Davis, Tone, or any of our great ones, and you will find them human, gay, and lovable. "Were you ever in love, Davis?" asked one of his wondering admirers, and prompt and natural came the reply: "I'm never out of it." We swear by Tone for his manly virtues; we love him because we say to ourselves: "What a fine fellow for a holiday." A friend of Mitchel's travelling with him once through a storm, was astonished to find him suddenly burst out into a fine recitation, which he delivered with fine effect. He was joyous in spirit. For their buoyancy we love them all, and because of it we emulate them. We are influenced, not by the man who always wants to preach a sermon at us, but by the one with whom we go for a holiday. Our history-makers were great, joyous men, of fine spirit, fine imagination, fine sensibility, and fine humour. They loved life; they loved their fellow man; they loved all the beautiful, brave things of earth. When you know them you can picture them scaling high mountains and singing from the summits, or boating on fine rivers in the sunlight, or walking about in the dawn, to the music of Creation, evolving the philosophy of revolutions and building beautiful worlds. You get no hint of this from the absurd propagandist play, yet this is what the heart of man craves. When he does not get it, he cannot explain what he wants; but he knows what he does not want, and he goes away and keeps his distance. The play has missed fire, and the playwright and his hero are ridiculous. Let us understand one thing: if we want to make men dutiful we must make them joyous.

IV

It is because we must talk of grave things that we must preserve our gaiety; otherwise we could not preserve our balance. By some freak of nature, the average man strikes attitudes as readily as the average boy whistles. We know how the *poseur* works mischief to every cause, and we can see the *poseur* on every side. In politics, he has made the platform contemptible, which is a danger to the nation, needing the right use of platform; in literature—well, we all know bourgeois, but who has done justice to the artist who gets on a platform to talk about the bourgeois?—in religion, the *poseur* is more likely to make agnostics than all the Rationalist Press; and the agnostic *poseur* in turn is very funny. Now all these are an affliction, a collection of absurdities of which we must cure the nation. If we cannot cure the nation of absurdity we cannot set her free. Let it be our rule to combine gaiety with gravity and we will acquire a saving sense of proportion. Only the solemn man is dull; the serious man has a natural fund of gaiety: we need only be natural to bring back joy to serious endeavour. Then we shall begin to move. Let us remember a revolution will surely fail when its leaders have no sense of humour.

V

But our humour will not be a saving humour unless it is of high order. A great humorist is as rare as a great poet or a great philosopher. Though ours may not be great we must keep it in the line of greatness. Remember, great humour must be made out of ourselves rather than out of others. The fine humorist is delightfully courteous; the commonplace wit, invariably insulting. We must keep two things in mind, that in laughter at our own folly is the beginning of wisdom; and the keenest wit is pure fun, never coarse fun. We start a laugh at others by getting an infallible laugh at ourselves. The commonplace wit arranges incidents to make someone he dislikes ridiculous; his attitude is the attitude of the superior person. He is nearly always—often unintentionally—offensive; he repels the public sometimes in irritation, sometimes in amusement, for they often see point in his joke, but see a greater joke in him, and they are often laughing, not at his joke, but at himself. Let us for our salvation avoid the attitude of the superior person. Don't make sport of others—make it of yourself. Ridicule of your neighbour must be largely speculation; of the comedy in yourself there can be no doubt. When you get the essential humour out of yourself, you get the infallible touch, and you arrest and attract everyone. You are not the superior person. In effect, you slap your neighbour on the back and say, "We're all in the same boat; let us enjoy the joke"; and you find he will come to you with glistening eye. He may feel a little foolish at first—you are poking his ribs; but you cannot help it—having given him the way to poke your own. By your merry honesty he knows you for a safe comrade, and he comes with relief and confidence—we like to talk about ourselves. He will be equally frank with yourself; you will tell one another secrets; you will reach the heart of man. That is what we need. We must get the heartbeat into literature. Then will it quiver and dance and weep and sing. Then we are in the line of greatness.

VI

It is because we need the truth that we object to the propagandist playwright. Only in a rare case does he avoid being partial; and when he is impartial he is cold and unconvincing. He gives us argument instead of emotion; but emotion is the language of the heart. He does not touch the heart; he tries to touch the mind: he is a pamphleteer and out of place. He fails, and his failure has damaged his cause, for it leaves us to feel that the cause is as cold as his play; but when the Cause is a great one it is always vital, warm and passionate. It is for the sake of the Cause we ask that a play be made by a sincere man-of-letters, who will give us not propagandist literature nor art-for-art's-sake, but the throbbing heart of man. The great dramatist will have the great qualities needed, sensibility, sympathy, insight, imagination, and courage. The special pleader and the *poseur* lack all these things, and they make themselves and their work foolish. Let us stand for the truth, not pruning it for the occasion. The man who is afraid to face life is not competent to lead anyone, to speak for anyone, or to interpret anything: he inspires no confidence. The one to rouse us must be passionate, and his passion will win us heart and soul. When from some terribly intense moment, he turns with a merry laugh, only the fool will take him as laughing at his cause; the general instinct will see him detecting an attitude, tripping it up, and making us all merry and natural again. In that moment we shall spring up astonished, enthusiastic, exultant—here is one inspired; we shall enter a passionate brotherhood, no cold disputes now—the smouldering fire along the land shall quicken to a blaze, history shall be again in the making. We shall be caught in the living flame.

CHAPTER XI

LITERATURE AND FREEDOM—ART FOR ART'S SAKE

I

Art for art's sake has come to have a meaning which must be challenged, but yet it can be used in a sense that is both high and sacred. If a gifted writer take literature as a great vocation and determine to use his talents faithfully and well, without reference to fee or reward; if prosperity cannot seduce him to the misuse of his genius, then we give him our high praise. Let it still not be forgotten that the labourer is worthy of his hire. But if the hire is not forthcoming, and he knowing it, yet says in his heart, "The work must still be done"; and if he does it loyally and bravely, despite the present coldness of the world, doing the good work for the love of the work and all beautiful things; and if with this meaning he take "art for art's sake" as his battle-cry, then we repeat it is used in a sense both high and sacred.

II

But there are artists abroad whose chief glory seems to be to deny that they have convictions—that is, convictions about the passionate things of life that rouse and move their generation. Now that they should not be special pleaders is an obvious duty, but unless they have a passionate feeling for the vital things that move men, heart and soul, they cannot interpret the heart and soul of passionate men, and their work must be for ever cold. When literature is not passionate it does not touch the spirit to lift and spread its wings and soar to finer air. That is the great want about all the clever books now being turned out—they often give us excitement; they never give us ecstasy. Then there is an obvious feeling of something lacking which men try to make up with art; and they produce work faultless in form and fastidious in phrase, but still it lacks the touch of fire that would lift it from common things to greatness.

III

If we are to apply art to great work we must distinguish art from artifice. We find the two well contrasted in Synge's "Riders to the Sea" and his "Playboy." The first was written straight from the heart. We feel Synge must have followed those people carrying the dead body, and touched to the quick by the *caoine*, passed the touch on to us, for in the lyric swell of the close we get the true emotion. Here alone is he in the line of greatness. This gripped his heart and he wrote out of himself. But in the other work of his it was otherwise. He has put his method on record: he listened through a chink in the floor, and wrote around other people. It is characteristic of the art of our time. Let it be called art if the critics will, but it is not life.

IV

No, it is not life. But there is so much talk just now of getting "down to fundamentals," of the poetry of the tramp "walking the world," and the rest of it, that it would be well if we *did get* down to fundamentals; and this is one thing fundamental—the tramp is a deserter from life. He evades the troubled field where great causes are fought; he shuns the battle because of the wounds and the sacrifice; he has no heart for high conflict and victory. Let him under the cover of darkness but secure his share of the spoils and the world may go to wreck. Yes, he is the meanest of things—a deserter. On the field of battle he would be shot. If we let him desert the field of life, go his way and walk the world, let us not at least hail him as a hero.

The Repertory Theatre is the nursery of this particular art-cult, and 'twould relieve some of us to talk freely about it. The Repertory Theatre has already become fashionable, and is quite rapidly become a nuisance. Men are making songs and plays and lectures for art's sake, for the praise of a coterie or to shock the bourgeois—above all shock the bourgeois. A certain type of artist delights in shocking the bourgeois—a riot over a play gives him great satisfaction. In passing, one must note with exasperation, perhaps with some misgiving, how men raise a riot over something not worth a thought, and will not fight for things for which they ought to die. But he likes the bourgeois to think him a terrible person; in his own esteem he is on an eminence, and he proceeds to send out more shock-the-bourgeois literature; and 'tis mostly very sorry stuff. Sometimes he tries to be emotional and is but painfully artificial; sometimes he tries to be merry and gives us flippancy for fun. And we feel a terrible need for getting back to a standard, worthy and true. Great work can be made only for the love of work; not for money, not for art's sake, not for intellectual appeal nor flippant ridicule, but for the pure love of things, good, true and beautiful. With the best of intentions we may fail; and this should be laid down as a safe guiding principle; a dramatist should be moved by his own tragedy; the novelist should be interested in his own story; the poet should make his song for the love of the song and his comedy for the fun of the thing.

VI

We naturally think of the Abbey Theatre when we speak of these things, and as the Abbey work has certainly suffered from overpraise we may correct it by comparison with Shakespeare. Before the Abbey we were so used to triviality that when clever and artistic work appeared we at once hailed it great. We *did* get one or two great things, a fact to note with hearty pleasure and pride. But the rest was merely clever; and now that we are getting nothing great we must insist, and keep on insisting, that 'tis merely clever. But let us remember that value of the word great. Let it be kept for such names as Shakespeare and Molière; and lesser men may be called brilliant, talented or able—anything you will but great. Consider the scenes from the supreme plays of Shakespeare and compare with them the innumerable plays now coming forth and note a vital difference. These give us excitement, where Shakespeare gave us vision. We may be reminded of Shakespeare's duels and brawls and battles and blood; his generation revelled in excitement. Yes, they craved it, and he gave it to them, but shot through with wonder, subtlety, ecstasy; and his splendid creations, like mighty worlds, keep us wondering for ever. We must get back that supreme note of blended music and wonder, that makes the spirit beautiful and tempts it to soar, till it rise over common things and mere commotion, spreading its wings for the finer air where reason faints and falls to earth.

VII

A dramatist cannot make a great play out of little people. His chief characters at least must be great of heart and soul—the great hearts that fight great causes. When such are caught, in the inevitable struggle of affections and duties and the general clash of life their passionate spirits send up all the elements that make great literature. The writer who cannot enter into their battles and espouse their cause cannot give utterance to their hearts; and we don't want what he thinks about them; we want what they think about themselves. He who is in passionate sympathy with them feels their emotion and writing from the heart does great things. The artist who is in mortal dread of being thought a politician or suspected of motives cannot feel, and will as surely fail, as the one who sits down to play the rôle of politician disguised as play-right. That is what the artist has got to see; and he has got to see that while the Irish Revolution for centuries has attracted the greatest hearts and brains of Ireland, for him carefully to avoid it is to avoid the line of greatness. For a propagandist to sit down to give it utterance would be as if a handy-man were to set out to build a cathedral. The Revolution does not need to be argued; it justifies itself—all we need is to give it utterance—give it utterance once greatly. Then the writer may proceed to give utterance to every good thing under the sun. But our artists are making, and will continue to make, only second-class literature, for they are afraid of the Revolution, and it is all over our best of life; they are afraid of that life. But to enter the arena of greatness they must give it a voice. That is the vocation of the poet.

VIII

Yes, and the poet will be unlike you, gentlemen of the fastidious phrase. He will not be careless of form, but the passion that is in him will make simple words burn and live; never will he in the mode of the time go wide of the truth to make a picturesque phrase; his mind rapt on the thing will fix on the true word; his heart warm with the battle will fashion more beautiful forms than you, O detached and dainty artist; his soul full of music and adventure will scale those heights it is your fate to dream of but not your fortune to possess. Yet, you, too, might possess them would you but step with him into the press of adventurous legions, and make articulate the dream of men, and make splendid their triumph. He is the prophet of to-morrow, though you deny him to-day. He is not like to you, supercilious and aloof—he would have you for a passionate brother, would raise your spirit in ecstasy, flood your mind with thought, and touch your lips with fire. Because of his sensitiveness he knows every mood and every heart and gives a voice and a song to all. You might know him for a good comrade, where freedom is to win or to hold, over in the van or the breach; able to deal good blows and take them in the fine manner, a fine fighter; not with darkened brow crying, "an eye for an eye"—for who *could* give him blow for blow or match his deed with a deed?—but one of open front and open hand who will count it happiness to have made for a victory he may not live to enjoy, as ready to die in its splendour as he had been to live through the darkness before the dawn; remembering with soldier tenderness the comrades of old battles, forgetting the malice of old enemies; a high example of the magnanimous spirit, happily not yet unknown on earth; with fine generosity and noble fire, full of that great love the common cry can never make other than humanising and beautiful, not without a gleam of humour more than half divine, he will pass, leaving to the foe that hated him heartily equally with the friend that loved him well, the wonder of his thought and the rapture of his melody.

CHAPTER XII

RELIGION

I

It ought to be laid down as a first principle that grave questions which have divided us in the past, and divide us still with much bitterness, should not be thrust aside and kept out of view in the hope of harmony. Where the attitude is such, the hope is vain. They should be approached with courage in the hope of creating mutual respect and an honourable solution for all. Religion is such a question. To the majority of men this touches their most intimate life. Because of their jealous regard for that intimate part of themselves they are prepared for bitter hostilities with anyone who will assail it; and because of the unmeasured bitterness of assaults on all sides we have come to count it a virtue to bring together in societies labelled non-sectarian, men who have been violently opposed on this issue. It will be readily allowed that to bring men together anyhow, even suspiciously, is somewhat of an advance, when we keep in mind how angrily they have quarrelled. But 'tis not to our credit that in any assembly a particular name hardly dare be mentioned; and it must be realised that, whatever purpose it may serve in lesser undertakings, in the great fight for freedom no such attitude will suffice. No grave question can be settled by ignoring it. Since it is our duty to make the War of Independence a reality and a success, we must invoke a contest that will as surely rouse every latent passion and give every latent suspicion an occasion and a field. That is the danger ahead. We must anticipate that danger, meet and destroy it. Perhaps at this suggestion most of us will at once get restive. Some may say with irritation: Why raise this matter? Others on the other side may prepare forthwith to dig up the hatchet. Is not the attitude on both sides evidence of the danger? Does anyone suppose we can start a fight for freedom without making that danger a grimmer reality? Who can claim it a wise policy merely for the moment to dodge it? For that is what we do. Let us have courage and face it. At what I have to say let no man take offence or fright—it commits no one to anything. It is written to try and make opponents understand and respect one another, not to set them at one another, least of all to make them "liberal," that is, lax and contemptible, ready to explain everything away. We want primarily the man who is prepared to fight his ground, but who is big enough in heart and mind to respect opponents who will also fight theirs. In the integrity and courage of both sides is the guarantee of the independence of both. That should be our guiding thought. But as on this question most people abandon all tolerance, it is quite possible what may be written will satisfy none; still, it may serve the purpose of making a need apparent. To repeat, we must face the question. But whoever elects to start it, should approach the issue with sympathy and forbearance. These are as necessary as courage and resolution; yet, since many often sacrifice firmness to sympathy, others will take the opposite line of riding roughshod over everyone, a harshness that confirms the weakling in his weakness. To note all this is but to note the difficulty; and if what is now written fails in its appeal, it need only be said to walk unerringly here would require the insight of a prophet and the balance of an angel.

II

What everyone should take as a fair demand is that all men should be sincere in their professions, and that we should justify ourselves by the consistency of our own lives rather than by the wickedness of our neighbours: which is nothing new. It is our trouble that we must emphasise obvious duties. To approach the question frankly with no matter what good faith will lead to much heart-burning, perhaps, to no little bitterness; but if we realise that all sides are about equally to blame, we may induce an earnestness that may lead to better things. It is in that hope I write. Catholics and Protestants, instead of saying to one another the things with which we are familiar, should look to their own houses; and if in this age of fashionable agnosticism, they should conclude that the general enemy is the atheist, socialist, and the syndicalist, they should still be reminded to look to their own houses; and if the agnostic take this to justify himself, he should be reminded he has never done anything to justify himself. It may seem a curious way for inducing harmony to set out to prove everyone in the wrong; but the point is clear, not to attack what men believe but to ask them to justify their words by their deeds. The request is not unreasonable and it may be asked in a tone that will show the sincerity of him who makes it and waken a kindred feeling in all earnest men. The world will be a better place to live in, and we shall be all better friends when every man makes a genuine resolve to give us all the example of a better life.

III

A development that would require a treatise in itself I will but touch on, to suggest to all interested a matter of general and grave concern—the growing materialism of religious bodies. On all sides self-constituted defenders of the faith are troubling themselves, not with the faith but with the numbers of their adherents who have jobs, equal sharers in emoluments, and so forth. A Protestant of standing writes a book and proves his religion is one of efficiency; a Catholic of equal standing quickly rejoins with another book to prove his religion is also efficient; each blind to the fact that the resulting campaign is disgraceful to both. When religion ceases to represent to us something spiritual, and purely spiritual, we begin to drift away from it. "Where thy treasure is, there thy heart is also." "No man can serve God and Mammon." The modern rejoinder is familiar: "We must live." This, our generation is not likely to forget. The grave concern is that well-meaning men are accustoming themselves to this cry to sacrifice all higher considerations for the "equal division of emoluments." Let us as citizens and a community see that every man has the right and the means to live; but when self-interested bodies start a rivalry in the name of their particular creeds, we know it ends in a squalid greed and fight for place, in a pursuit of luxury, the logical outcome of which must be to make the world ugly, sordid and brutal. It would be a mistake to overlook that high-minded men are allowing themselves to be committed by plausible reasons to this growing evil. It is misguided enthusiasm. There is a divine authority that warns us all: "Be zealous for the better gifts."

IV

I wish to examine the attitude of the average Christian to the Agnostic. "The world is falling away from religion," he will cry when depressed, without thinking how much he himself may be a contributing cause. Let him study it in this light. What is his attitude? When he comes to speak of the tendency of the age he will indulge in vague generalities about atheism, socialism, irreligion, and the rest; always the cause is outside of him, and against him; he is not part of it. I ask him to pass by the atheist awhile and take what may be of more concern. There is a type of Catholic and Protestant who has as little genuine religion in him as any infidel, who does not deny the letter of the law, but who does not observe its spirit, whose only use for the letter is to criticise and harass adversaries. Observe the high use he has for liberty—drinking, card-playing, gambling, luxury; he has no place in his life for any worthy deeds, nay, only scorn for such. Still he passes for orthodox. If he is a Catholic, he secures that by putting in an appearance at Mass on Sundays. His mind is not there; he arrives late and goes early. His Protestant fellow in his private judgment finds more scope: "Let the women go listen to the parson." This is the sort of saying gives him such a conceit of himself. We have the type on both sides, so all can see it. Now it is not in the way of the Pharisee we come to note them, but to note that, strange as it may appear, either or both together will come to applaud the denouncing of the atheist. We gather such into our religious societies, and flatter them that they are adherents of religion and the bulwark of the faith, and they forthwith anathematise the atheist with great gusto. The one so anathematised is often as worthless as themselves with a conceit to despise priest and parson alike. But it sometimes happens he is a fine character who has no religion as most of us understand it, but who has yet a fine spiritual fervour, ready to fight and make sacrifices for a national or social principle that he believes will make for better things, a man of integrity and worth whom the best of men may be glad to hold as a friend. Yet we find in the condition to which we have drifted such a one may be pilloried by wasters, gamblers, rioters, a crew that are the curse of every community. We lash the atheist and the age but give little heed to the insincerity and cant of those we do not refuse to call our own. What an example for the man anathematised. He sees the vice and meanness of those we allow to pass for orthodox, and when he sees also the complacency of the better part, he is unconvinced. We praise the sweetness of the healing waters of Christ-like charity, but despite our gospel he never gets it, never. We give him execration, injustice; if we let him go with a word, it is never a gentle word, but a bitter epithet; and we wonder he is estranged, when he sees our amazing composure in an amazing welter of hypocrisy and deceit. There is, of course, the better side, the many thousands of Catholics and Protestants who sincerely aim at better things. But what has to be admitted is that most sincerely religious people adopt to the man of no established religion the same attitude as does the hypocrite: they join in the general cry. They should look to their own houses; they should purge the temple of the money-lender and the knave; they should see that their field gives good harvest; they should remember that not to the atheist only but to the orthodox was it written: "Every tree therefore that doth not yield good fruit shall be cut down and cast into the fire."

V

There is a word to be said to the man for whom was invented the curious name agnostic. I'm concerned only with him who is sincere and high-minded. Let us pass the flippant critics of things they do not understand. But all sincere men are comrades in a deep and fine sense. What the honest unbeliever has to keep in mind is that the darker side is but one side. If he stands studying a crowd of the orthodox and finds therein the drunkard, the gambler, the sensualist; and if he says bitter things of the value of religion and gets in return the clerical fiat of one who is more a politician than a priest; and if he rejoins contemptuously, "This is fit for women and children," let him be reminded that he can also study the other side if he care. If he has the instinct of a fighter he must know every army has in its trail the camp-follower and the vulture, but when the battle is set and the danger is imminent, only the true soldier stands his ground. Because some who are of poor spirit are in high place, let him not forget the old spirit still exists. Not only the women but the best intellects of men still keep the old traditions. Newman and Pascal, Dante and Milton, Erigena and Aquinas, are all dead, but in our time even they have had followers not too far off. In the same spirit Gilbert Chesterton found wonder at a wooden post, and Francis Thompson, in his divine wandering, troubled the gold gateways of the stars. Let our friend before he frames his final judgment pause here. He may well be baffled by many anomalies of the time, his eye may rest on the meaner horde, his ear be filled with the arrogance of some unworthy successor of Paul; and if he says: "Why permit these things?" he may be told there are some alive in this generation who will question all such things, and who, however hard it go with them, have no fear for the final victory.

VI

Perhaps the conventional Christian and conventional non-Christian may rest a moment to consider the reality. Between the bitter believer and the exasperated unbeliever, Christianity is being turned from a practice to a polemic, and if we are to recall the old spirit we must recall the old earnestness and simplicity of the early Martyrs. We do not hear that they called Nero an atheist, but we do hear that they went singing to the arena. By their example we may recover the spirit of song, and have done with invective. If we find music and joyousness in the old conception, it is not in the fashion of the time to explain it away in some "new theology," for he to whom it is not a fashion, but a vital thing, keeps his anchor by tradition. To him it is the shining light away in the mists of antiquity; it is the strong sun over the living world; it is the pillar of fire over the widening seas and worlds of the unknown; it is the expanse of infinity. When he is lost in its mystery he adverts to the wonder about him, for all that is wonderful is touched with it, and all that is lovely is its expression. It is in the breath of the wind, pure and bracing from the mountain top. It is in the song of the lark holding his musical revel in the sunlight. It is in the ecstasy of a Spring morning. It is in the glory of all beautiful things. When it has entered and purified his spirit, his heart goes out to the persecuted in all ages and countries. None will he reject. "I am not come to call the just but sinners." He remembers those words, and his great charity encompasses not only the persecuted orthodox, but the persecuted heretics and infidels.

VII

I will not say if such an endeavour as I suggest can have an immediate success. But I think it will be a step forward if we get sincere men on one side to understand the sincerity of the other side; and if in matters of religion and speculation, where there is so much difficulty and there is likely to be so much conflict of opinion, there should be no constraint, but rather the finest charity and forbearance; then the orthodox would be concerned with practising their faith rather than in harassing the infidel, and the infidel would receive a more useful lesson than the ill-considered tirades he despises. He may remain still unconvinced, but he will give over his contempt. This question of religion is one on which men will differ, and differing, ultimately they will fight if we find no better way. We must remember while freedom is to win we are facing a national struggle, and if we are threatened within by a civil war of creeds it may undo us. That is why we must face the question. That is why I think utter frankness in these grave matters is of grave urgency. If we approach them in the right spirit we need have no fear—for at heart the most of men are susceptible to high appeals. What we need is courage and intensity; it is gabbling about surface things makes the bitterness. If in truth we safeguard the right of every man as we are bound to do we shall win the confidence of all, and we may hope for a braver and better future, wherein some light of the primal Beauty may wander again over earth as in the beginning it dawned on chaos when the Spirit of God first moved over the waters.

CHAPTER XIII

INTELLECTUAL FREEDOM

I

It will probably cause surprise if I say there is, possibly, more intellectual freedom in Ireland than elsewhere in Europe. But I do not mean by intellectual freedom conventional Free-thought, which is, perhaps, as far as any superstition from true freedom of the mind. The point may not be admitted but its consideration will clear the air, and help to dispose of some objections hindering that spiritual freedom, fundamental to all liberty.

II

I have no intention here of in any way criticising the doctrine of Free-thought, but one so named cannot be ignored when we consider Intellectual Freedom. This, then, has to be borne in mind when speaking of Free-thought, that while it allows you latitude of opinion in many things, it will not allow you freedom in all things, in, for example, Revealed Religion. I only mention this to show that on both sides of such burning questions you have disputants dogmatic. A dogmatic "yes" meets an equally dogmatic "no." The dogmas differ and it is not part of our business here to discuss them: but to come to a clear conception of the matter in hand, it must be kept in mind, that if you, notwithstanding, freely of your own accord, accept belief in certain doctrines, the freethinkers will for that deny you freedom. And the freethinkers are right in that they are dogmatic. (But this they themselves appear to overlook.) Freedom is absolutely dogmatic. It is fundamentally false that freedom implies no attachment to any belief, no being bound by any law, "As free as the wind," as the saying goes, for the wind is not free. Simple indeterminism is not liberty.

III

We must, then, find the true conception of Intellectual Freedom. It is the freedom of the individual to follow his star and reach his goal. That star binds him down to certain lines and his freedom is in exact proportion to his fidelity to the lines. The seeming paradox may be puzzling: a concrete example will make it clear. Suppose a man, shipwrecked, finds himself at sea in an open boat, without his bearings or a rudder. He is at the mercy of the wind and wave, without freedom, helpless. But give him his bearings and a helm, and at once he recovers his course; he finds his position and can strike the path to freedom. He is at perfect liberty to scuttle his boat, drive it on the rocks or do any other irrational thing; but if he would have freedom, he must follow his star.

IV

This leads us to track a certain error that has confused modern debate. A man in assumed impartiality tells you he will stand away from his own viewpoint and consider a case from yours. Now, if he does honestly hold by his own view and thinks he can put it by and judge from his opponent's, he is deceiving both himself and his opponent. He can do so *apparently*, but, whatever assumption is made, he is governed subconsciously by his own firm conviction. His belief is around him like an atmosphere; it goes with him wherever he goes; he can only stand free of it by altogether abandoning it. If his case is such that he can come absolutely to the other side to view it uninfluenced by his own, then he has abandoned his own. He is like a man in a boat who has thrown over rudder and bearings: he may be moved by any current: he is adrift. If he is to recover the old ground, he must win it as something he never had. But if instead of this he does at heart hold by his own view, he should give over the deception that he is uninfluenced by it in framing judgment. It is psychologically impossible. Let the man understand it as a duty to himself to be just to others, and to substitute this principle for his spurious impartiality. This is the frank and straightforward course. While he is under his own star, he is moving in its light: he has, if unconsciously, his hand on the helm: he judges all currents scrupulously and exactly, but always from his own place at the wheel and with his own eyes. To abandon one or the other is to betray his trust, or in good faith and ignorance to cast it off till it is gone, perhaps, too far to recover.

V

If we so understand intellectual freedom, in what does its denial consist? In this: around every set of principles guiding men, there grows up a corresponding set of prejudices that with the majority in practice often supersede the principles; and these prejudices with the march of time assume such proportions, gather such power, both by the numbers of their adherents and the authority of many supporting them, that for a man of spirit, knowing them to be evil and urgent of resistance, there is needed a vigour and freedom of mind that but few understand and even fewer appreciate or encourage. The prejudices that grow around a man's principles are like weeds and poison in his garden: they blight his flowers, trees and fruit; and he must go forth with fire and sword and strong unsparing hand to root out the evil things. He will find with his courage and strength are needed passion and patience and dogged persistence. For men defend a prejudice with bitter venom altogether unlike the fire that quickens the fighter for freedom; and the destroyer of the evil may find himself assailed by an astonishing combination—charged with bad faith or treachery or vanity or sheer perversity, in proportion as those who dislike his principles deny his good faith; or those who profess them, because of his vigour and candour denounce him for an enemy within the fold. But for all that he should stand fast. If he has the courage so to do, he gives a fine example of intellectual freedom.

VI

It will serve us to consider some prejudices, free-thinking and religious. First the free-thinker. He has a prejudice very hard to kill. If I believe in the beginning what Bernard Shaw has found out thus late in the day, that priests are not as bad as they are painted, the free-thinker would deny me intellectual freedom. The fact of my right to think the matter out and come to that conclusion would count for nothing. On the other hand, if I were known to have professed a certain faith and to have abandoned it, he would acclaim that as casting off mental slavery. This is hopelessly confusing. If a man has ceased to hold a certain belief he deserves no credit for courage in saying so openly. If he thinks what he once believed, or is supposed to have believed, has no vitality, surely he can have no reason for being afraid of it, and to speak of dangerous consequences from it to him, can be *for him* at least only a bogey. His simple denial is, then, no mark of courage. Courage is a positive thing. Yet he may well have that courage. Suppose him in taking his stand to have taken up some social faith that for him has promise of better things. He will find his new creed surrounded by its own swarm of prejudices, and if he refuse to worship every fetish of the free-thinker, declaring that this stands to him for a certain definite, beautiful thing, and fighting for it, he will find himself denied and scouted by his new friends. He may find himself often in company with some supposed enemies. He will surely need in his sincere attitude to life a freedom of mind that is not a name merely but a positive virtue that demands of him more than denunciation of obscurantism, the recognition of a personal duty and the justification of personal works.

VII

The religious prejudice will be no less hard to kill. Indiscriminate denunciation of unbelievers as wicked men serves no good purpose and leads nowhere. There are wicked men on all sides. Our standard must be one that will distinguish the sincere men on all sides; and our loyalty to our particular creeds must be shown in our lives and labours, not in the reviling of the infidel. We are justified in casting out the hypocrite from every camp, and when we come to this task we can be sure only of the hypocrites in our own; and we should lay it as an injunction on all bodies to purge themselves. The burden will be laid on all—not one surely of which men can complain—that they shall prove their principles in action and lay their prejudices by. Christians might well find exemplars in the early martyrs, those who for their principles went so readily to the lions. One may anticipate the complacent rejoinder: "This is not so exacting an age; men are not asked to die for religion now"—and one may in turn reply, that, perhaps our age may not be without occasion for such high service, but that we may be unwilling to go to the lions. Our time has its own trial—by no means unexacting let me tell you—but we quietly slip it by: it is much easier to revile the infidel. This as a test of loyalty should be pinned: we shall shut up thereby the hypocrite. And the earnest man, more conscious of his own burden, will be more sympathetic, generous and just, and will come to be more logical and to see what Newman well remarked, that one who asks questions shows he has no belief and in asking may be but on the road to one. If to ask a question is to express a doubt, it is no less, perhaps, to seek a way out of it. "What better can he do than inquire, if he is in doubt?" asks Newman. "Not to inquire is in his case to be satisfied with disbelief." We should, acting in this light, instead of denouncing the questioner, answer his question freely and frankly, encourage him to ask others and put him one or two by the way. Men meeting in this manner may still remain on opposite sides, but there will be formed between them a bond of sympathy that mutual sincerity can never fail to establish. This is freedom, and a fine beautiful thing, surely worth a fine effort. What we have grown accustomed to, the bitterness, the recriminations, the persecutions and retaliations, are all the evil weeds of prejudice, growing around our principles and choking them. They are so far a denial of principle, a proof of mental slavery. Our freedom will attest to faith: "Where the Spirit of the Lord is, there is Liberty."

VIII

This, in conclusion, is the root of the matter: to claim freedom and to allow it in like measure; rather than to deny, to urge men to follow their beliefs: only thus can they find salvation. To constrain a man to profess what we profess is worse than delusion: should he give lip service to what he does not hold at heart, 'twere for him deceitful and for us dangerous. Where his star calls, let him walk sincerely. If his creed is insufficient or inconsistent, in his struggle he shall test it, and in his sincerity he must make up the insufficiency or remove the inconsistency. This is the only course for honourable men and no man should object. To repeat, it puts an equal burden on all—the onus of justifying the faith that is in them. Life is a divine adventure and he whose faith is finest, firmest and clearest will go farthest. God does not hold his honours for the timid: the man who buried his talent, fearing to lose it, was cast into exterior darkness. He who will step forward fearlessly will be justified. "All things are possible to him who believeth." Many on both sides may be surprised to find suddenly proposed as a test to both sides the readiness to adventure bravely on the Sea of Life. The free-thinker may be astonished to hear, not that he goes too far, but does not go far enough. He may gasp at the test, but it is in effect the test and the only true one. The man who does not believe he is to be blotted out when his body ceases to breathe, who holds all history for his heritage and the wide present for his battle-ground, believes also the future is no repellent void but a widening and alluring world. If in his travel he is scrupulous in detail, it is in the spirit of the mariner who will neither court a ship-wreck nor be denied his adventure. He cannot deny to others the right to hesitate and halt by the way, but his spirit asks no less than the eternal and the infinite. Yes, but many good religious people are not used to seeing the issue in this light, and those who make a trade of fanning old bitterness will still ply their bitter trade, crying that anarchists, atheists, heretics, infidels, all outcasts and wicked men, are all rampant for our destruction. It may be disputed, but, admitting it, one may ask: Is there no place among Christian people for those distinctive virtues on which we base the superiority of our religion? When the need is greatest, should the practice be less urgent? It is not evident that the free-thinker is obliged by any of his principles to give better example. It is evident the Christian is so obliged. Why is he found wanting? If human weakness were pleaded, one could understand. It is against the making a virtue of it lies the protest. How many noble things there are in our philosophies, and how little practised. No violent convulsions should be needed to make us free, if men were but consistent: we should find ourselves wakening from a wicked dream in a bloodless and beautiful revolution. We are in the desert truly and a long way from the Promised Land. But we must get to the higher ground and consider our position; and if one by one we are stripped of the prejudices that too long have usurped the place of faith, and we find ourselves, to our dismay, perhaps lacking that faith that we have so long shouted but so little testified, and tremble on the verge of panic, there is one last line that gives in four words with divine simplicity and completeness a final answer to all timidity and objections: "Fear not; only believe."

CHAPTER XIV

MILITARISM

I

To defend or recover freedom men must be always ready for the appeal to arms. Here is a principle that has been vindicated through all history and needs vindication now. But in our time the question of rightful war has been crossed by the evil of militarism, and in our assertion of the principle, that in the last resort freemen must have recourse to the sword, we find ourselves crossed by the anti-militarist campaign. We must dispose of this confusing element before we can come to the ethics of war. Of the evil of militarism there can be no question, but a careful study of some anti-militaristic literature discloses very different motives for the campaign. I propose to lay some of the motives bare and let the reader judge whether there may not be an insidious plot on foot to make a deal between the big nations to crush the little ones. For this purpose I will consider two books on the question, one by Mr. Norman Angell, "The Great Illusion," and one by M. Jacques Novikow, "War and Its Alleged Benefits." In the work of Mr. Angell the reader will find the suggestion of the deal, while in the work of M. Novikow is given a clear and honest statement of the anti-militarist position, with which we can all heartily agree. Those of us who would assert our freedom should understand the right anti-militarist position, because in its exponents we shall find allies at many points. But with Mr. Angell's book it is otherwise. These points emerge: the basis of morality is self-interest; the Great Powers have nothing to gain by destroying one another, they should agree to police and exploit the territory of the "backward races"; if the statesmen take a different view from the financiers, the financiers can bring pressure to bear on the statesmen by their international organisation; the capitalist has no country. Well, our comment is, the patriot has a country, and when he wakens to the new danger, he may spoil the capitalist dream, and this book of Mr. Angell's may in a sense other than that the author intended be appropriately named "The Great Illusion."

II

The limits of this essay do not admit of detailed examination of the book named. What I propose to do is make characteristic extracts sufficiently full to let the reader form judgment. As we are only concerned for the present with the danger I mention, I take particular notice of Mr. Angell's book, and I refer the reader for further study to the original. But the charge of taking an accidental line from its context cannot be made here, as the extracts are numerous, the tendency of all alike, and more of the same nature can be found. I divide the extracts into three groups, which I name:

1. The Ethics of the Case.

2. The Power of Money.

3. The Deal.

Where italics are used they are mine.

> 1. THE ETHICS OF THE CASE.—"The real basis of Social Morality is self-interest." ("The Great Illusion," 3rd Ed., p. 66.) "Have we not abundant evidence, indeed, that the passion of patriotism, as divorced from material interest, is being modified by the pressure of material interest?" (p. 167.) "Piracy was magnificent, doubtless, but it was not business." (Speaking of the old Vikings, p. 245.) "The pacifist propaganda has failed largely because it has not put (and proven) the plea of interest as distinct from the moral plea." (p. 321.)
>
> 2. THE POWER OF MONEY.—"The complexity of modern finance makes New York dependent on London, London upon Paris, Paris upon Berlin, to a greater degree> than has ever yet been the case in history." (p. 47.)
>
> "It would be a miracle if already at this point the whole influence of British Finance were not thrown against the action of the British Government." (On the assumed British capture of Hamburg, p. 53).
>
> "The most absolute despots cannot command money." (p. 226.)
>
> "With reference to capital, it may almost be said that it is organised so naturally internationally that *formal organisation is not necessary.*" (p. 269.)
>
> 3. THE DEAL.—"France has benefited by the conquest of Algeria, England by that of India, because in each case the arms were employed not, properly speaking, for conquest at all, but *for police purposes.*" (p. 115.)
>
> "While even the wildest Pan-German has never cast his eyes in the direction of Canada, he has cast them, and does

cast them, in the direction of Asia Minor.... *Germany may need to police Asia Minor.*" (pp. 117, 118.)

"*It is much more to our interest to have an orderly and organised Asia Minor under German tutelage than to have an unorganised and disorderly one which should be independent.*" (p. 120.)

"Sir Harry Johnston, in the 'Nineteenth Century' for December, 1910, comes a great deal nearer to touching the real kernel of the problem.... He adds that the best informed Germans used this language to him: '*You know that we ought to make common cause in our dealings with backward races of the world!*'"

The quotations speak for themselves. Note the policing of the "backward races." The Colonies are not in favour. Mr. Angell writes: "What in the name of common sense is the advantage of conquering them if the only policy is to let them do as they like?" (p. 92.) South Africa occasions bitter reflections: "The present Government of the Transvaal is in the hands of the Boer Party." (p. 95.) And he warns Germany, that, supposing she wishes to conquer South Africa, "she would learn that the policy that Great Britain has adopted was not adopted by philanthropy, but in the hard school of bitter experience." (p. 104.) We believe him, and we may have to teach a lesson or two in the same school. It may be noted in passing Mr. Angell gives Ireland the honour of a reference. In reply to a critic of the *Morning Post*, who wrote thus: "It is the sublime quality of human nature that every great nation has produced citizens ready to sacrifice themselves rather than submit to external force attempting to dictate to them a conception other than their own of what is right." (p. 254.) Mr. Angell replied: "One is, of course, surprised to see the foregoing in the *Morning Post*; the concluding phrase would justify the present agitation in India, or in Egypt, or in Ireland against British, rule." (p. 254.) Comment is needless. The reading and re-reading of this book forces the conclusion as to its sinister design. Once that design is exposed its danger recedes. There is one at least of the "backward races" that may not be sufficiently alive to self-interest, but may for all that upset the capitalist table and scatter the deal by what Ruskin described in another context as "the inconvenience of the reappearance of a soul."

III

We must not fail to distinguish the worth of the best type of anti-militarist and to value the truth of his statement. It is curious to find Mr. Angell writing an introduction to M. Novikow's book, for M. Novikow's position is, in our point of view, quite different. He does not draw the fine distinction of policing the "backward races." Rather, he defends the

Bengalis. Suppose their rights had never been violated, he says: "They would have held their heads higher; they would have been proud and dignified, and perhaps might have taken for their motto, *Dieu et mon droit*." ("War and Its Alleged Benefits," p. 12.) He can be ironical and he can be warm. Later, he writes; "The French (and all other people) should vindicate their rights with their last drop of blood; so what I write does not refer to those who defend their rights, but to those who violate the rights of others." (Note p. 70.) He does not put by the moral plea, but says: "Political servitude develops the greatest defects in the subjugated peoples." (p. 79.) And he pays his tribute to those who die for a noble cause: "My warmest sympathy goes out to those noble victims who preferred death to disgrace." (p. 82.) This is the true attitude and one to admire; and any writer worthy of esteem who writes for peace never fails to take the same stand. Emerson, in his essay on "War," makes a fine appeal for peace, but he writes: "If peace is sought to be defended or preserved for the safety of the luxurious or the timid, it is a sham and the peace will be base. War is better, and the peace will be broken." And elsewhere on "Politics," he writes: "A nation of men unanimously bent on freedom or conquest can easily confound the arithmetic of the statists and achieve extravagant actions out of all proportions to their means." Yes, and by our unanimity for freedom we mean to prove it true.

CHAPTER XV

THE EMPIRE

I

With the immediate promise of Home Rule many strange apologists for the Empire have stepped into the sun. Perhaps it is well—we may find ourselves soon more directly than heretofore struggling with the Empire. So far the fight has been confused. Imperialists fighting for Home Rule obscured the fact that they were *not* fighting the Empire. Now Home Rule is likely to come, and it will serve at least the good purpose of clearing the air and setting the issue definitely between the nation and the Empire. We shall have our say for the nation, but as even now many things, false and hypocritical, are being urged on behalf of the Empire, it will serve us to examine the Imperial creed and show its tyranny, cruelty, hypocrisy, and expose the danger of giving it any pretext whatever for aggression. For the Empire, as we know it and deal with it, is a bad thing in itself, and we must not only get free of it and not be again trapped by it, but must rather give hope and encouragement to every nation fighting the same fight all the world over.

II

One candid writer, Machiavelli, has put the Imperial creed into a book, the examination of which will—for those willing to see—clear the air of illusion. Now, we are conscious that defenders of the Empire profess to be shocked by the wickedness of Machiavelli's utterance—we shall hear Macaulay later—but this shocked attitude won't delude us. Let those who have not read Machiavelli's book, "The Prince," consider carefully the extracts given below and see exactly how they fit the English occupation of Ireland, and understand thoroughly that the Empire is a thing, bad in itself, utterly wicked, to be resisted everywhere, fought without ceasing, renounced with fervour and without qualification, as we have been taught from the cradle to renounce the Devil with all his works and pomps. Consider first the invasion. Machiavelli speaks:—"The common method in such cases is this. As soon as a foreign potentate enters into a province those who are weaker or disobliged join themselves with him out of emulation and animosity to those who are above them, insomuch that in respect to those inferior lords no pains are to be omitted that may gain them; and when gained, they will readily and unanimously fall into one mass with the State that is conquered. Only the conqueror is to take special care that they grow not too strong, nor be entrusted with too much authority, and then he can easily with his own forces and their assistance keep down the greatness of his neighbours, and make himself absolute arbiter in that province." Here is the old maxim, "Divide and conquer." To gain an entry some pretence is advisable. Machiavelli speaks with approval of a certain potentate who always made religion a pretence. Having entered a vigorous policy must be pursued. We read—"He who usurps the government of any State is to execute and put in practice all the cruelties which he thinks material at once." Cromwell rises before us.

"A prince," says Machiavelli, "is not to regard the scandal of being cruel if thereby he keeps his subjects in their allegiance." "For," he is cautioned, "whoever conquers a free town and does not demolish it commits a great error and may expect to be ruined himself; because whenever the citizens are disposed to revolt they betake themselves, of course, to that blessed name of Liberty, and the laws of their ancestors, which no length of time nor kind usage whatever will be able to eradicate." An alternative to utter destruction is flattery and indulgence. "Men are either to be flattered and indulged or utterly destroyed." We think of the titles and the bribes. Again, "A town that has been anciently free cannot more easily be kept in subjection than by employing its own citizens." We think of the place-hunter, the King's visit, the "loyal" address. To make the conquest secure we read: "When a prince conquers a new State and annexes it as a member to his old, then it is necessary your subjects be disarmed, all but such as appeared for you in the conquest, and they are to be mollified by degrees and brought into such a condition of laziness and effeminacy that in time your whole strength may devolve upon your own natural militia." We think of the Arms Acts and our weakened people. But while one-half is disarmed and the other half bribed, with neither need the conqueror keep faith. We read: "A prince who is wise and prudent cannot, or ought not, to keep his parole, when the keeping of it is to his prejudice and the causes for which he promised removed." This is made very clear to prevent any mistake. "It is of great consequence to disguise your inclination and play the hypocrite well." We think of the Broken Treaty and countless other breaches of faith. It is, of course, well to seem honourable, but Machiavelli cautions: "It is honourable to seem mild, and merciful, and courteous, and religious, and sincere, and indeed to be so, provided your mind be so rectified and prepared, that you can act quite contrary upon occasion." Should anyone hesitate at all this let him hear: "He is not to concern himself if run under the infamy of those vices, without which his dominion was not to be preserved." Thus far the philosophy of Machiavelli. The Imperialist out to "civilise the barbarians" is, of course, shocked by such wickedness; but we are beginning to open our eyes to the wickedness and hypocrisy of both. To us this book reads as if a shrewd observer of the English Occupation in Ireland had noted the attending features and based these principles thereon.

We have reason to be grateful to Machiavelli for his exposition. His advice to the prince, in effect, lays bare the marauders of his age and helps us to expose the Empire in our own.

III

There is a lesson to be learnt from the fact that this book of Machiavelli's, written four centuries ago in Italy, is so apt here to-day. We must take this exposition as the creed of Empire and have no truck with the Empire. It may be argued that the old arts will be no longer practised on us. Let the new supporters of the Empire know that by the new alliance they should practise these arts on other people, which would be infamy. We are not going to hold other people down; we are going to encourage them to stand up. If it means a further fight we have plenty of stimulus still. Our oppression has been doubly bitter for having been mean. The tyranny of a strong mind makes us rage, but the tyranny of a mean one is altogether insufferable. The cruelty of a Cromwell can be forgotten more easily than the cant of a Macaulay. When we read certain lines we go into a blaze, and that fire will burn till it has burnt every opposition out. In his essay on Milton, Macaulay having written much bombast on the English Revolution, introduces this characteristic sentiment: "One part of the Empire there was, so unhappily circumstanced, that at that time its misery was necessary to our happiness and its slavery to our freedom." For insolence this would be hard to beat. Let it be noted well. It is the philosophy of the "Predominant Partner." If he had thanked God for having our throats to cut, and cut them with loud gratitude like Cromwell, a later generation would be incensed. But this other attitude is the gall in the cup. Macaulay is, of course, shocked by Machiavelli's "Prince." In his essay on Machiavelli we read: "It is indeed scarcely possible for any person not well acquainted with the history and literature of Italy to read without horror and amazement the celebrated treatise which has brought so much obloquy on the name of Machiavelli. Such a display of wickedness, naked, yet not ashamed, such cool, judicious, scientific atrocity, seemed rather to belong to a fiend than to the most depraved of men." But, later, in the same essay, is a valuable sidelight. He writes of Machiavelli as a man "whose only fault was that, having adopted some of the maxims then generally received, he arranged them most luminously and expressed them more forcibly than any other writer." Here we have the truth, of course not so intended, but evident: Machiavelli's crime is not for the sentiments he entertained but for writing them down luminously and forcibly—in other words, for giving the show away.

Think of Macaulay's "horror and amazement," and read this further in the same essay: "Every man who has seen the world knows that nothing is so useless as a general maxim. If it be very moral and very true it may serve for a copy to a charity boy." So the very moral and the very true are not for the statesman but for the charity-boy. This perhaps may be defended as irony; hardly, but even so, in such irony the character appears as plainly as in volumes of solemn rant. To us it stands out clearly as the characteristic attitude of the English Government. The English people are used to it, practise it, and will put up with it; but the Irish people never were, are not now, and never will be used to it; and we won't put up with it. We get calm as old atrocities recede into history, but to repeat the old cant, above all to try and sustain such now, sets all the old fire blazing—blazing with a fierceness that will end only with the British connection.

IV

Not many of us in Ireland will be deceived by Macaulay, but there is danger in an occasional note of writers, such as Bernard Shaw and Stuart Mill. Our instinct often saves us by natural repugnance from the hypocrite, when we may be confused by some sentiment of a sincere man, not foreseeing its tendency. When an aggressive power looks for an opening for aggression it first looks for a pretext, and our danger lies in men's readiness to give it the pretext. Such a sentiment as this from Mill—on "Liberty"—gives the required opening: "Despotism is a legitimate mode of government in dealing with Barbarians, provided the end be their improvement"; or this from Shaw's preface to the Home Rule edition of "John Bull's Other Island": "I am prepared to Steam-roll Tibet if Tibet persist in refusing me my international rights." Now, it is within our right to enforce a principle within our own territory, but to force it on other people, called for the occasion "barbarians," is quite another thing. Shaw may get wrathful, and genuinely so, over the Denshawai horror, and expose it nakedly and vividly as he did in his first edition of "John Bull's Other Island," Preface for Politicians; but the aggressors are undisturbed as long as he gives them pretexts with his "steam-roll Tibet" phrase. And when he says further that he is prepared to co-operate with France, Italy, Russia, Germany and England in Morocco, Tripoli, Siberia and Africa to civilise these places, not only are his denunciations of Denshawai horrors of no avail—except to draw tears after the event—but he cannot co-operate in the civilising process without practising the cruelty; and perhaps in their privacy the empire-makers may smile when Shaw writes of Empire with evident earnestness as "a name that every man who has ever felt the sacredness of his own native soil to him, and thus learnt to regard that feeling in other men as something holy and inviolable, spits out of his mouth with enormous contempt." When, further, in his "Representative Government" Mill tells the English people—a thing about which Shaw has no illusions—that they are "the power which of all in existence best understands liberty, and, whatever may have been its errors in the past, has attained to more of conscience and moral principle in its dealing with foreigners than any other great nation seems either to conceive as possible or recognise as desirable"—they not only go forward to civilise the barbarians by Denshawai horrors, but they do so unctuously in the true Macaulayan style. We feel a natural wrath at all this, not unmingled with amusement and amazement. In studying the question we read much that rouses anger and contempt, but one must laugh out heartily in coming to this gem of Mill's, uttered with all Mill's solemnity: "Place-hunting is a form of ambition to which the English, considered nationally, are almost strangers." When the sincerest expression of the English mind can produce this we need to have our wits about us; and when, as just now, so much nonsense, and dangerous nonsense, is being poured abroad about the Empire, we need to pause, carefully consider all these things, and be on our guard.

V

In conclusion, we may add our own word to the talk of the hour—the politicians on Home Rule. It should raise a smile to hear so often the prophecy that Ireland will be loyal to the Empire when she gets Home Rule. We are surprised that any Irishman could be so foolish, though, no doubt, many Englishmen are so simple as to believe it. History and experience alike deny it. Possibly the Home Rule chiefs realise their active service is now limited to a decade or two, and assume Home Rule may be the limit for that time, and speak only for that time; but at the end of that time our generation will be vigorous and combative, and if we cannot come into our own before then, we shall be ready then. We need say for the moment no more than this—the limit of the old generation is not the limit of ours. If anyone doubt the further step to take let him consider our history, recent and remote. The old effort to subdue or exterminate us having failed, the new effort to conciliate us began. Minor concessions led to the bigger question of the land. One Land Act led to another till the people came by their own. Home Rule, first to be killed by resolute government, was next to be killed by kindness, and Local Government came. Local Government made Home Rule inevitable; and now Home Rule is at hand and we come to the last step. Anyone who reads the history of Ireland, who understands anything of progress, who can draw any lesson from experience, must realise that the advent of Home Rule marks the beginning of the end.

CHAPTER XVI

RESISTANCE IN ARMS—FOREWORD

I

The discussion of freedom leads inevitably to the discussion of an appeal to arms. If proving the truth and justice of a people's claim were sufficient there would be little tyranny in the world, but a tyrannical power is deaf to the appeal of truth—it cannot be moved by argument, and must be met by force. The discussion of the ethics of revolt is, then, inevitable.

II

The ubiquitous pseudo-practical man, petulant and critical, will at once arise: "What is the use of discussing arms in Ireland? If anyone wanted to fight it would be impossible, and no one wants to fight. What prevents ye going out to begin?" Such peevish criticism is anything but practical, and one may ignore it; but it suggests the many who would earnestly wish to settle our long war with a swift, conclusive fight, yet who feel it no longer practical. Keeping to the practical issue, we must bear in mind a few things. Though Ireland has often fought at odds, and could do so again, it is not just now a question of Ireland poorly equipped standing up to England invincible. England will never again have such an easy battle. The point now to emphasise is this—by remaining passive and letting ourselves drift we drift into the conflict that involves England. We must fight for her or get clear of her. There can be no neutrality while bound to her; so a military policy is an eminently practical question. Moreover, it is an urgent one: to stand in with England in any danger that threatens her will be at least as dangerous as a bold bid to break away from her. One thing above all, conditions have changed in a startling manner; England is threatened within as without; there are labour complications of all kinds of which no one can foresee the end, while as a result of another complication we find the Prime Minister of England going about as carefully protected as the Czar of Russia.[Footnote: The militant suffragette agitation.] The unrest of the times is apt to be even bewildering. England is not alone in her troubles—all the great Powers are likewise; and it is at least as likely for any one of them to be paralysed by an internal war as to be prepared to wage an external one. This stands put clearly—we cannot go away from the turmoil and sit down undisturbed; we must stand in and fight for our own hand or the hand of someone else. Let us prepare and stand for our own. However it be, no one can deny that in all the present upheavals it is at least practical to discuss the ethics of revolt.

III

We can count on a minority who will see wisdom in such a discussion; it must be our aim to make the discussion effective. We must be patient as well as resolute. We are apt to get impatient and by hasty denunciation drive off many who are wavering and may be won. These are held back, perhaps, by some scruple or nervousness, and by a fine breath of the truth and a natural discipline may yet be made our truest soldiers. Emerson, in his address at the dedication of the Soldiers' Monument, Concord, made touching reference in some such in the American Civil War. He told of one youth he knew who feared he was a coward, and yet accustomed himself to danger, by forcing himself to go and meet it. "He enlisted in New York," says Emerson, "went out to the field, and died early." And his comment for us should be eloquent. "It is from this temperament of sensibility that great heroes have been formed." The pains we are at to make men physically fit we must take likewise to make them mentally fit. We are minutely careful in physical training, drill regulations and the rest, which is right, for thus we turn a mob into an army and helplessness into strength. Let us be minutely careful, too, with the untried minds—timid, anxious, sensitive in matters of conscience; like him Emerson spoke of, they may be found yet in the foremost fighting line, but we must have patience in pleading with them. Here above all must we keep our balance, must we come down with sympathy to every particular. It is surely evident that it is essential to give the care we lavish on the body with equal fulness to the mind.

IV

At the heart of the question we will be met by the religious objection to revolt. Here all scruples, timidity, wavering, will concentrate; and here is our chief difficulty to face. The right to war is invariably allowed to independent states. The right to rebel, even with just cause, is not by any means invariably allowed to subject nations. It has been and is denied to us in Ireland. We must answer objectors line by line, leading them, where it serves, step by step to our conclusions; but this is not to make freedom a mere matter of logic—it is something more. When it comes to war we shall frequently give, not our promises, but our conclusions. This much must be allowed, however, that, as far as logic will carry, our position must be perfectly sound; yet, be it borne in mind, our cause reaches above mere reasoning—mere logic does not enshrine the mysterious touch of fire that is our life. So, when we argue with opponents we undertake to give them as good as or better than they can give, but we stake our cause on the something that is more. On this ground I argue not in general on the right of war, but in particular on the right of revolt; not how it may touch other people elsewhere ignoring how it touches us here in Ireland. A large treatise could be written on the general question, but to avoid seeming academic I will confine myself as far as possible to the side that is our concern. For obvious reasons I propose to speak as to how it affects Catholics, and let them and others know what some Catholic writers of authority have said on the matter. One thing has to be carefully made clear. It is seen in the following quotation from an eminent Catholic authority writing in Ireland in the middle of the last century, Dr. Murray, of Maynooth: "The Church has issued no definition whatever on the question—has left it open. Many theologians have written on it; the great majority, however (so far as I have been able to examine them), pass it over in silence." (*Essays chiefly Theological*, vol. 4). This has to be kept in mind. Theologians have written, some on one side and some on the other, but the Church has left it open. I need not labour the point why it is useful to quote Catholic authorities in particular, since in Ireland an army representative of the people would be largely Catholic, and much former difficulty arose from Catholics in Ireland meeting with opposition from some Catholic authorities. It may be seen the position is delicate as well as difficult, and in writing a preliminary note one point should be emphasised. We must not evade a difficulty because it is delicate and dangerous, and we must not temporise. In a physical contest on the field of battle it is allowable to use tactics and strategy, to retreat as well as advance, to have recourse to a ruse as well as open attack; but *in matters of principle there can be no tactics, there is one straightforward course to follow, and that course must be found and followed without swerving to the end.*

CHAPTER XVII

RESISTANCE IN ARMS—THE TRUE MEANING OF LAW

I

When we stand up to question false authority we should first make our footing firm by showing we understand true authority and uphold it. Let us be clear then as to the meaning of the word law. It may be defined; an ordinance of reason, the aim of which is the public good and promulgated by the ruling power. Let us cite a few authorities. "A human law bears the character of law so far as it is in conformity with right reason; and in that point of view it is manifestly derived from the Eternal Law." (*Aquinas Ethicus*, Vol. 1, p. 276.) Writing of laws that are unjust either in respect to end, author or form, St. Thomas says: "Such proceedings are rather acts of violence than laws; because St. Augustine says: 'A law that is not just goes for no law at all.'" (*Aquinas Ethicus*, Vol. 1, p. 292.) "The fundamental idea of all law," writes Balmez, "is that it be in accordance with reason, that it be an emanation from reason, an application of reason to society" (*European Civilisation*, Chap. 53). In the same chapter Balmez quotes St. Thomas with approval: "The kingdom is not made for the king, but the king for the kingdom"; and he goes on to the natural inference: "That all governments have been established for the good of society, and that this alone should be the compass to guide those who are in command, whatever be the form of government." It is likewise the view of Mill, in *Representative Government*, that the well-being of the governed is the sole object of government. It was the view of Plato before the Christian era: his ideal city should be established, "that the whole City might be in the happiest condition." (*The Republic*, Book 4.) Calderwood writes: "Political Government can be legitimately constructed only on condition of the acknowledgment of natural obligations and rights as inviolable." (*Handbook of Modern Philosophy, Applied Ethics*, Sec. 4.) Here all schools and all times are in agreement. Till these conditions are fulfilled for us we are at war. When an independent and genuine Irish Government is established we shall yield it a full and hearty allegiance: the law shall then be in repute. We do not stand now to deny the idea of authority, but to say that the wrong people are in authority, the wrong flag is over us.

II

"We must overthrow the arguments that might be employed against us by the advocates of blind submission to any power that happens to be established," writes Balmez, on resistance to *De Facto* Governments.

(*European Civilisation*, Chap. 55.) We could not be more explicit than the famous Spanish theologian. To such arguments let the following stand out from his long and emphatic reply:—"Illegitimate authority is no authority at all; the idea of power involves the idea of right, without which it is mere physical power, that is force." He writes further: "The conqueror, who, by mere force of arms, has subdued a nation, does not thereby acquire a right to its possession; the government, which by gross iniquities has despoiled entire classes of citizens, exacted undue contributions, abolished legitimate rights, cannot justify its acts by the simple fact of its having sufficient strength to execute these iniquities." There is much that is equally clear and definite. What extravagant things can be said on the other side by people in high places we know too well. Balmez in the same book and chapter gives an excellent example and an excellent reply: "Don Felix Amat, Archbishop of Palmyra, in the posthumous work entitled *Idea of the Church Militant*, makes use of these words: 'Jesus Christ, by His plain and expressive answer, *Render to Cæsar the things that are Cæsar's*, has sufficiently established that the mere fact of a government's existence is sufficient for enforcing the obedience of subjects to it....' His work was forbidden at Rome," is Balmez' expressive comment, and he continues, "and whatever may have been the motives for such a prohibition, we may rest assured that, in the case of a book advocating such doctrines, every man who is jealous of his rights might acquiesce in the decree of the Sacred Congregation." So much for *De Facto* Government. It is usurpation; by being consummated it does not become legitimate. When its decrees are not resisted, it does not mean we accept them in principle—nor can we even pretend to accept them—but that the hour to resist has not yet come. It is the strategy of war.

III

We stand on the ground that the English Government in Ireland is founded in usurpation and as such deny its authority. But if it be argued, assuming it as Ireland's case, that a usurped authority, gradually acquiesced in by the people, ultimately becomes the same as legitimate, the reply is still clear. For ourselves we meet the assumption with a simple denial, appealing to Irish History for evidence that we never acquiesced in the English Usurpation. But to those who are not satisfied with this simple denial, we can point out that even an authority, originally founded legitimately, may be resisted when abusing its power to the ruin of the Commonwealth. We still stand on the ground that the English government is founded in usurpation, but we can dispose of all objections by proving the extremer case. This is the case Dr. Murray, already quoted, discusses. "The question," he writes, "is about resistance to an established and legitimate government which abuses its power." (*Essays, Chiefly Theological*, Vol. 4.) He continues: "The common opinion of a large number of our theologians, then, is that it is lawful to resist by force, and if necessary to depose, the sovereign ruler or rulers, in the extreme—the very extreme—case wherein the following conditions are found united:

> "1. The tyranny must be excessive—intolerable.
>
> "2. The tyranny must be manifest, manifest to men of good sense and right feeling.
>
> "3. The evils inflicted by the tyrant must be greater than those which would ensue from resisting and deposing him.
>
> "4. There must be no other available way of getting rid of the tyranny except by recurring to the extreme course.
>
> "5. There must be a moral certainty of success.
>
> "6. The revolution must be one conducted or approved by the community at large ... the refusal of a small party in the State to join with the overwhelming mass of their countrymen would not render the resistance of the latter unlawful." (*Essays, Chiefly Theological*; see also Rickaby, *Moral Philosophy*, Chap. 8, Sec. 7.)

Some of these conditions are drawn out at much length by Dr. Murray. I give what is outstanding. How easily they could fit Irish conditions must strike anyone. I think it might fairly be said that our leaders generally would, if asked to lay down conditions for a rising, have framed some more stringent than these. It might be said, in truth, of some of them that they seem to wait for more than a moral certainty of success, an absolute certainty, that can never be looked for in war.

IV

When a government through its own iniquity ceases to exist, we must, to establish a new government on a true and just basis, go back to the origin of Civil Authority. No one argues now for the Divine Right of Kings, but in studying the old controversy we get light on the subject of government that is of all time. To the conception that kings held their power immediately from God, "Suarez boldly opposed the thesis of the initial sovereignty of the people; from whose consent, therefore, all civil authority immediately sprang. So also, in opposition to Melanchthon's theory of governmental omnipotence, Suarez *a fortiori* admitted the right of the people to depose those princes who would have shown themselves unworthy of the trust reposed in them." (De Wulf, *History of Medieval Philosophy*, Third Edition, p. 495.) Suarez' refutation of the Anglican theory, described by Hallam as clear, brief, and dispassionate, has won general admiration. Hallam quotes him to the discredit of the English divines: "For this power, by its very nature, belongs to no one man but to a multitude of men. This is a certain conclusion, being common to all our authorities, as we find by St. Thomas, by the Civil laws, and by the great canonists and casuists; all of whom agree that the prince has that power of law-giving which the people have given him. And the reason is evident, since all men are born equal, and consequently no one has a political jurisdiction over another, nor any dominion; nor can we give any reason from the nature of the thing why one man should govern another rather than the contrary." (Hallam—*Literature of Europe*, Vol. 3, Chap. 4.) Dr. Murray, in the essay already quoted, speaks of Sir James Mackintosh as the ablest Protestant writer who refuted the Anglican theory, which Mackintosh speaks of as "The extravagance of thus representing obedience as the only duty without an exception." Dr. Murray concludes his own essay on *Resistance to the Supreme Civil Power* by a long passage from Mackintosh, the weight and wisdom of which he praises. The greater part of the passage is devoted to the difficulties even of success and emphasising the terrible evils of failure. In what has already been written here I have been at pains rather to lay bare all possible evils than to hide them. But when revolt has become necessary and inevitable, then the conclusion of the passage Dr. Murray quotes should be endorsed by all: "An insurrection rendered necessary by oppression, and warranted by a reasonable probability of a happy termination, is an act of public virtue, always environed with so much peril as to merit admiration." Yes, and given the happy termination, the right and responsibility of establishing a new government rest with the body of the people.

V

We come, then, to this conclusion, that government is just only when rightfully established and for the public good; that usurpation not only may but ought to be resisted; that an authority originally legitimate once it becomes habitually tyrannical may be resisted and deposed; and that when from abuse or tyranny a particular government ceases to exist, we have to re-establish a true one. It is sometimes carelessly said, "Liberty comes from anarchy," but this is a very dangerous doctrine. It would be nearer truth to say from anarchy inevitably comes tyranny. Men receive a despot to quell a mob. But when a people, determined and disciplined, resolve to have neither despotism nor anarchy but freedom, then they act in the light of the Natural Law. It is well put in the doctrine of St. Thomas, as given by Turner in his *History of Philosophy* (Chap. 38): "The redress to which the subjects of a tyrant have a just right must be sought, not by an individual, but by an authority temporarily constituted by the people and acting according to law." Yes, and when wild and foolish people talk hysterically of our defiance of all authority, let us calmly show we best understand the basis of Authority—which is Truth, and most highly reverence its presiding spirit—which is Liberty.

CHAPTER XVIII

RESISTANCE IN ARMS—OBJECTIONS

I

Having stated the case for resistance, it will serve us to consider some objections. Many inquiring minds may be made happy by a clear view of the doctrine, till some clever opponent holds them up with remarks on prudence, possibly sensible, or remarks on revolutionists, most probably wild, with, perhaps, the authority of a great name, or unfailing refuge in the concrete. It is curious that while often noticed how men, trying to evade a concrete issue, take refuge in the abstract, it is not noticed that men, trying to avoid acknowledging the truth of some principle, take refuge in the concrete. A living and pressing difficulty, though transient, looms larger than any historical fact or coming danger. Seeing this, we may restore confidence to a baffled mind, by helping it to distinguish the contingent from the permanent. Thus, by disposing of objections, we make our ground secure.

II

To the name of prudence the most imprudent people frequently appeal. Those whose one effort is to evade difficulties, who to cover their weakness plead patience, would be well advised to consider how men passionately in earnest, enraged by these evasions, pour their scorn on patience as a thing to shun. The plea does not succeed; it only for the moment damages the prestige of a great name. Patience is not a virtue of the weak but of the strong. An objector says: "Of course, all this is right in the abstract, but consider the frightful abuses in practice," and some apt replies spring to mind. Dr. Murray, writing on "Mental Reservation," in his *Essays, chiefly Theological*, speaks thus: "But it is no objection to any principle of morals to say that unscrupulous men will abuse it, or that, if publicly preached to such and such an audience or in such and such circumstances, it will lead to mischief." This is admirable, to which the objector can only give some helpless repetitions. With Balmez, we reply: "But in recommending prudence to the people let us not disguise it under false doctrines—let us beware of calming the exasperation of misfortune by circulating errors subversive of all governments, of all society." (*European Civilisation*, Chap. 55.) Of men who shrink from investigating such questions, Balmez wrote: "I may be permitted to observe that their prudence is quite thrown away, that their foresight and precaution are of no avail. Whether they investigate these questions or not, they *are* investigated, agitated and decided, in a manner that we must deplore." (Ibid. Chap. 54.) Take with this Turner on France under the old *régime* and the many and serious grievances of the people: "The Church, whose duty it was to inculcate justice and forbearance, was identified, in the minds of the people, with the Monarchy which they feared and detested." (*History of Philosophy*, Chap. 59.) The moral is that when injustice and evil are rampant, let us have no palliation, no weakness disguising itself as a virtue. What we cannot at once resist, we can always repudiate. To ignore these things is the worst form of imprudence—an imprudence which we, for our part at least, take the occasion here heartily to disclaim.

III

There is so much ill-considered use of the word revolutionist, we should bear in mind it is a strictly relative term. If the freedom of a people is overthrown by treachery and violence, and oppression practised on their once thriving land, that is a revolution, and a bad revolution. If, with tyranny enthroned and a land wasting under oppression, the people rise and by their native courage, resource and patience re-establish in their original independence a just government, that is a revolution, and a good revolution. The revolutionist is to be judged by his motives, methods and ends; and, when found true, his insurrection, in the words of Mackintosh, is "an act of public virtue." It is the restoration of, Truth to its place of honour among men.

IV

Balmez mentions Bossuet as apparently one who denies the right here maintained; and we may with profit read some things Bossuet has said in another context, yet which touches closely what is our concern. Writing of *Les Empires*, thus Bossuet: "Les révolutions des empires sont réglées par la providence, et servent à humilier les princes." This is hardly calculated to deter us from a bid for freedom; and if we go on to read what he has written further under this heading, we get testimony to the hardihood and love of freedom and country that distinguished early Greece and Rome in language of eloquence that might inflame any people to liberty. Of undegenerate Greece, free and invincible: "Mais ce que la Grece avait de plus grand était une politique ferme et prévoyante, qui savait abandonner, hasarder et défendre, ce qu'il fallait; et, ce qui est plus grand encore, un courage que l'amour de la liberté et celui de la patrie rendaient invincible." Of undegenerate Rome, her liberty: "La liberté leur était donc un trésor qu'ils préferoient à toutes les richesses de l'univers." Again: "La maxime fondamentale de la république était de regarder la liberté comme une chose inséparable du nom Roman." And her constancy: "Voila de fruit glorieux de la patience Romaine. Des peuples qui s'enhardissaient et se fortifiaient par leurs malheurs avaient bien raison de croire qu'on sauvait tout pourvu qu'on ne perdît pas l'esperance." And again: "Parmi eux, dans les états les plus tristes, jamais les faibles conseils n'ont été seulement écoutés." The reading of such a fine tribute to the glory of ancient liberties is not likely to diminish our desire for freedom; rather, to add to the natural stimulus found in our own splendid traditions, the further stimulus of this thought that must whisper to us: "Persevere and conquer, and to-morrow our finest opponent will be our finest panegyrist when the battle has been fought and won."

V

In conclusion, in the concrete this simple fact will suffice: we have established immutable principles; the concrete circumstances are contingent and vary. It is admirably put in the following passage: "The historical and sociological sciences, so carefully cultivated in modern times, have proved to evidence that social conditions *vary* with the epoch and the country, that they are the resultant of quite a number of fluctuating influences, and that, accordingly, the science of Natural Right should not merely establish *immutable* principles bearing on the moral end of man, but should likewise deal with the *contingent* circumstances accompanying the application of those principles." (De Wulf, *Scholasticism, Old and New*, Part 2, Chap. 2, Sec. 33.) Yes, and if we apply principles to-morrow, it is not with the conditions of to-day we must deal, but "with the contingent circumstances accompanying the application of those principles." Let that be emphasised. The conditions of twenty years ago are vastly changed to-day; and how altered the conditions of to-morrow can be, how astonishing can be the change in the short span of twenty years, let this fact prove. Ireland in '48 was prostrate after a successful starvation and an unsuccessful rising—to all appearances this time hopelessly crushed; yet within twenty years another rising was planned that shook English government in Ireland to its foundations. Let us bear in mind this further from De Wulf: "Sociology, understood in the wider and larger sense, is transforming the methods of the science of Natural Right." In view of that transformation he is wise who looks to to-morrow. What De Wulf concludes we may well endorse, when he asks us to take facts as they are brought to light and study "each question on its merits, in the light of these facts and not merely in its present setting but as presented in the pages of history." It can be fairly said of those who have always stood for the separation of Ireland from the British Empire, that they alone have always appealed to historical evidence, have always regarded the conditions of the moment as transient, have always discussed possible future contingencies. The men who temporised were always hypnotised by the conditions of the hour. But in the life-story of a nation stretching over thousands of years, the British occupation is a contingent circumstance, and the immutable principle is the Liberty of the Irish People.

CHAPTER XIX

THE BEARNA BAOGHAIL—CONCLUSION

I

But when principles have been proved and objections answered, there are still some last words to say for some who stand apart—the men who held the breach. For, they do stand apart, not in error but in constancy; not in doubt of the truth but its incarnation; not average men of the multitude for whom human laws are made, who must have moral certainty of success, who must have the immediate allegiance of the people. For it is the distinguishing glory of our prophets and our soldiers of the forlorn hope, that the defeats of common men were for them but incentives to further battle; and when they held out against the prejudices of their time, they were not standing in some new conceit, but most often by prophetic insight fighting for a forgotten truth of yesterday, catching in their souls to light them forward, the hidden glory of to-morrow. They knew to be theirs by anticipation the general allegiance without which lesser men cannot proceed. They knew they stood for the Truth, against which nothing can prevail, and if they had to endure struggle, suffering and pain, they had the finer knowledge born of these things, a knowledge to which the best of men ever win—that if it is a good thing to live, it is a good thing also to die. Not that they despised life or lightly threw it away; for none better than they knew its grandeur, none more than they gloried in its beauty, none were so happily full as they of its music; but they knew, too, the value of this deep truth, with the final loss of which Earth must perish: the man who is afraid to die is not fit to live. And the knowledge for them stamped out Earth's oldest fear, winning for life its highest ecstasy. Yes, and when one or more of them had to stand in the darkest generation and endure all penalties to the extreme penalty, they knew for all that they had had the best of life and did not count it a terrible thing if called by a little to anticipate death. They had still the finest appreciation of the finer attributes of comradeship and love; but it is part of the mystery of their happiness and success, that they were ready to go on to the end, not looking for the suffrage of the living nor the monuments of the dead. Yes, and when finally the re-awakened people by their better instincts, their discipline, patriotism and fervour, will have massed into armies, and marched to freedom, they will know in the greatest hour of triumph that the success of their conquering arms was made possible by those who held the breach.

II

When, happily, we can fall back on the eloquence of the world's greatest orator, we turn with gratitude to the greatest tribute ever spoken to the memory of those men to whom the world owes most. Demosthenes, in the finest height of his finest oration, vindicates the men of every age and nation who fight the forlorn hope. He was arraigned by his rival, Æschines, for having counselled the Athenians to pursue a course that ended in defeat, and he replies thus: "If, then, the results had been foreknown to all—not even then should the Commonwealth have abandoned her design, if she had any regard for glory, or ancestry, or futurity. As it is, she appears to have failed in her enterprise, a thing to which all mankind are liable, if the Deity so wills it." And he asks the Athenians: "Why, had we resigned without a struggle that which our ancestors encountered every danger to win, who would not have spit upon you?" And he asks them further to consider strangers, visiting their City, sunk in such degradation, "especially when in former times our country had never preferred an ignominious security to the battle for honour." And he rises from the thought to this proud boast: "None could at any period of time persuade the Commonwealth to attach herself in secure subjection to the powerful and unjust; through every age has she persevered in a perilous struggle for precedency and honour and glory." And he tells them, appealing to the memory of Themistocles, how they honoured most their ancestors who acted in such a spirit: "Yes; the Athenians of that day looked not for an orator or a general, who might help them to a pleasant servitude: they scorned to live if it could not be with freedom." And he pays them, his listeners, a tribute: "What I declare is, that such principles are your own; I show that before my time such was the spirit of the Commonwealth." From one eloquent height to another he proceeds, till, challenging Æschines for arraigning him, thus counselling the people, he rises to this great level: "But, never, never can you have done wrong, O Athenians, in undertaking the battle for the freedom and safety of all: I swear it by your forefathers—those that met the peril at Marathon, those that took the field at Plataea, those in the sea-fight at Salamis, and those at Artimesium, and many other brave men who repose in the public monuments, all of whom alike, as being worthy of the same honour, the country buried, Æschines, not only the successful and victorious." We did not need this fine eloquence to assure us of the greatness of our O'Neills and our Tones, our O'Donnells and our Mitchels, but it so quickens the spirit and warms the blood to read it, it so touches—by the admiration won from ancient and modern times—an enduring principle of the human heart—the capacity to appreciate a great deed and rise over every physical defeat—that we know in the persistence of the spirit we shall come to a veritable triumph. Yes; and in such light we turn to read what Ruskin called the greatest inscription ever written, that which Herodotus tells us was raised over the Spartans, who fell at Thermopylæ, and which Mitchel's biographer quotes as most fitting to epitomise Mitchel's life: "Stranger, tell thou the Lacedemonians that we are lying here, having obeyed their words." And the biographer of Mitchel is right in holding that he who reads into the significance of these brave lines, reads a message not of defeat but of victory.

III

Yes; and in paying a fitting tribute to those great men who are our exemplars, it would be fitting also, in conclusion, to remember ourselves as the inheritors of a great tradition; and it would well become us not only to show the splendour of the banner that is handed on to us, but to show that this banner *we*, too, are worthy to bear. For, how often it shall be victorious and how high it shall be planted, will depend on the conception we have of its supreme greatness, the knowledge that it can be fought for in all times and places, the conviction that we may, when least we expect, be challenged to deny it; and that by our bearing we may bring it new credit and glory or drag it low in repute. We do well, I say, to remember these things. For in our time it has grown the fashion to praise the men of former times but to deny their ideal of Independence; and we who live in that ideal, and in it breathe the old spirit, and preach it and fight for it and prophesy for it an ultimate and complete victory—we are young men, foolish and unpractical. And what should be our reply? A reply in keeping with the flag, its history and its destiny. Let them, who deride or pity us, see we despise or pity their standards, and let them know by our works—lest by our election they misunderstand—that we are not without ability in a freer time to contest with them the highest places—avoiding the boast, not for an affected sense of modesty but for a saving sense of humour. For in all the vanities of this time that make Life and Literature choke with absurdities, pretensions and humbug, let us have no new folly. Let us with the old high confidence blend the old high courtesy of the Gaedheal. Let us grow big with our cause. Shall we honour the flag we bear by a mean, apologetic front? No! Wherever it is down, lift it; wherever it is challenged, wave it; wherever it is high, salute it; wherever it is victorious, glorify and exult in it. At all times and forever be for it proud, passionate, persistent, jubilant, defiant; stirring hidden memories, kindling old fires, wakening the finer instincts of men, till all are one in the old spirit, the spirit that will not admit defeat, that has been voiced by thousands, that is noblest in Emmet's one line, setting the time for his epitaph: "*When* my country"—not *if*—but "*when* my country takes her place among the nations of the earth." It is no hypothesis; it is a certainty. There have been in every generation, and are in our own, men dull of apprehension and cold of heart, who could not believe this, but we believe it, we live in it: *we know it*. Yes, we know it, as Emmet knew it, and as it shall be seen to-morrow; and when the historian of to-morrow, seeing it accomplished, will write its history, he will not note the end with surprise. Rather will he marvel at the soul in constancy, rivalling the best traditions of undegenerate Greece and Rome, holding through disasters, persecutions, suffering, and not less through the seductions of milder but meaner times, seeing through all shining clearly the goal: he will record it all, and, still marvelling, come to the issue that dauntless spirit has reached, proud and happy; but he will write of that issue—*Liberty; Inevitable*: in two words to epitomise the history of a people that is without a parallel in the Annals of the World.